ALLY PALLY

The Alexandra Palace — Its Transport & Its Troubles

C. T. GOODE

Forge Books

Published by Forge Books,
42, Rectory Lane, Bracknell
Berkshire.
1983

ISBN 0 904662 12 8

Photoset in Imprint 10/11
Produced by Alan Sutton Publishing Limited, Gloucester
Printed in Great Britain by Redwood Burn Ltd, Trowbridge

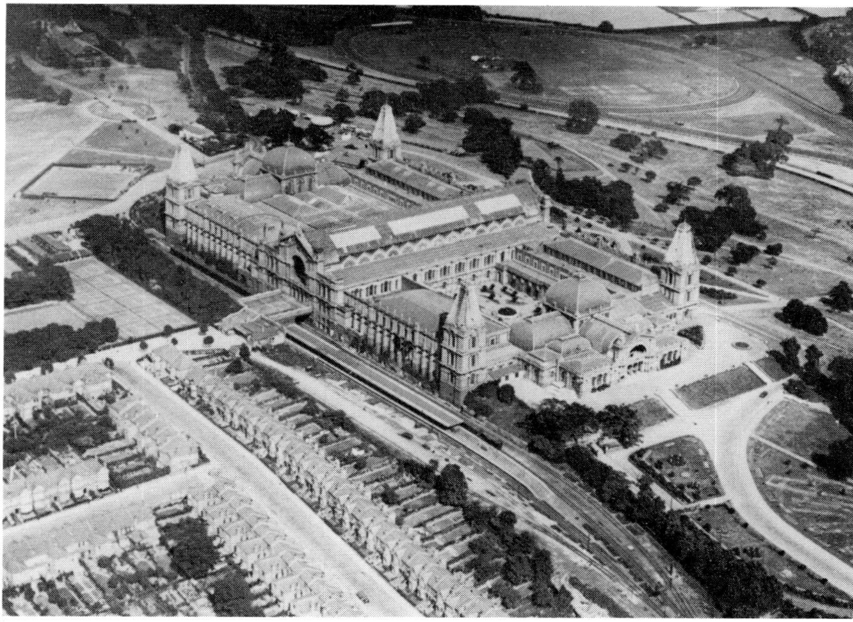

Introduction

I must admit that, for many years, I believed in all youthful innocence that Alexandra Palace was, as its name so conveniently suggested, the royal home of Alexandra, though what that lady might have done with her husband Edward while she was in residence there never crossed my mind.

For those speeding into Kings Cross from the north, the grey structure on the hill to the right is the harbinger of that spirit of London, that essence which greets one on leaving the train. 'Crystal Palace!' someone in the know cries, causing some confusion. 'No it isn't, it's that place where the BBC do things'. Thus the Palace stolidly stands surveying the not particularly imposing scene below it and sharpening the wits of the multitudes hurrying through Wood Green.

In its heyday, almost all London must have visited the Palace and Park, certainly the latter, and few would have lavished praise on the vast structure which was already out-of-date from that moment it was built as a poor replica of what seemed a finer assemblage of rooms and galleries. Over the years, like a materfamilias, it has been expected to perform well the duties demanded of it, with little praise and less reward. Woodwork has perished, guttering unwisely constructed of zinc has rotted, allowing the damp to attack the walls, and glass has loosened in places with disastrous results. People who should have known better have come and vandalised and gone. The mater-familias has become dowdy. However, one warms to those moments of glory in wartime, a period which, paradoxically, brings out the best in most of us, when the Palace mothered many refugees and gave a lodging to the goods and chattels from local households ravaged by Hitler's bombs.

In a world where Temples of Sport burgeon in almost every town and village nowadays, it would appear that Alexandra Palace and Park have a real chance to serve the last years of this century and even further ahead. Sadly, many of those who visit now use their own transport, but for the connoisseur of nostalgia, five minutes spent just off the North Terrace near to the old station building, which still survives, will rouse the ghosts of greater days when thousands of eager visitors would arrive by train upon train.

I should like to acknowledge the kind assistance given to me by Mr. Hart of the Greater London Council Library, by Miss Pegram of Bruce Castle Museum, Tottenham who took great trouble to unearth much useful information, by the staff of the Public Record Office, Kew, and by the Librarians of the Royal Institutes of Civil Engineers and British Architects. F.J. Mackett A.R.I.B.A. gave valuable help with the architectural sections.

C. Tony Goode, Anlaby,
Hull.

The First Structure

The Alexandra Palace and the railway which served it each has a history almost equally interesting. The idea of a park and palace of recreation and entertainment for the general public grew up in the wake of the success which the Crystal Palace enjoyed after its transfer to Sydenham Hill, south of London, following the Great Exhibition in Hyde Park of 1851. The Prince Consort died in 1861, and a second Great Exhibition was held one year later in Cromwell Road, South Kensington. What, then, could be a more natural corollary than the suggestion of a group of businessmen that something similar should be done to house many of the delights of that exhibition, and that a worthy structure should be built north of the city to benefit those who lived there and save them the journey across the capital, one which was often tedious and complicated. Therefore, all the useful materials and structures were salvaged from the second Great Exhibition and earmarked for re-erection on Muswell Hill, an eminence of 310 ft. and 240 acres situated west of Hornsey and New Southgate. The original architect of the 1862 Exhibition was Captain Francis Fowke, RE, designer of much of the Victoria and Albert Museum.

The Park came first, opened by Alexandra, Princess of Wales attending a Flower Show on 23rd. July 1863. Not everyone was in favour of the idea. One letter written at the time welcomed the initiative shown by the Alexandra Palace Company, but wondered whether the local footpaths were not too important to be given up without some equivalent. Tolls had already been charged for some time for the use of existing footpaths, and one in particular was threatened with closure, namely that from the Colney Hatch road just beyond Wood Green, over the Great Northern Railway's main line and up to the High Road at the top of Muswell Hill. Tolls would prevent some of the poorer people from enjoying the beautiful view, and to avoid them would involve a long detour by way of Hornsey and Colney Hatch.

The original prospectus for the project was published on 13th November 1858, which was in fact well in advance of the second Exhibition itself. It stated that the idea was to erect on Muswell Hill a kind of Crystal Palace for the inhabitants of the north of London, but that 'the objects set forth were to be less than one half the cost of the Crystal Palace at Sydenham.'

Wood Green station on the Great Northern main line was opened on 1st. May 1859 and seems to have been erected as a result of a contribution of £4,000 by the developers of the Tottenham Wood estate, part of which was in turn developed into the pleasure park. A spur line was originally intended to leave the main route at the north end of Wood Green, with attendant flying junctions, however, that particular idea was not proceeded with at the outset, though the project was to be raised again later.

After the Park was opened, the Race Course followed in 1868, whilst the construction of the Palace began in 1864. The building was designed by J. Johnson, Architect, and M. Meeson, Engineer, the builders being Messrs. Kelk and Lucas. Some there were who would have liked to have named the Palace after the late Prince Albert, but this was not desirable as his name had already been bestowed on the Albert Hall. Attention therefore turned to the newly married Alexandra Princess of Wales, the eldest daughter of King Christian IX of Denmark and future Queen of Edward VII.

The contractors had a large force of about one thousand workmen employed on site in the construction of the Palace, with many more off the site constructing the various interior fittings. The building consisted of a central portion or nave, 900 ft. long by 80 ft. wide with a centre transept of 430 ft. and two shorter transepts of 320 ft. each, all of 85 ft. width and intersecting three domes were erected, that in the centre being the one used at the Great Exhibition of 1862, a mighty affair 220 ft. high inside and 170 ft. in diameter but with the bottom two thirds of the original glazing replaced with solid roofing and internal panelling.

The ends of the nave and transepts were furnished with large rose windows fitted with stained glass. Each of the ends, eight in all, had pedimented facades and arcaded entrances.

'Above the roofs there rises in the centre a bold tambour, twelve sided, pierced with windows and surmounted with a cornice and entablature, from which springs the great dome, which is terminated at the top by a balustraded parapet and a standard mast 80 ft. in height. This great dome is covered with Muntz's brass coloured metal, laid on with a lap and tongue in a peculiar manner and panelled in relief by moulded ribs. The octagon cupolas at the intersections of the smaller transepts and nave show also above the roof noble tambours, with entablature and cornice, and an Italian roof, covered by zinc in rools, and terminated by an ornamental finial, which will be gilt. On all sides of the building are formed terraces, which will be laid out with much taste; on these terraces and the adjoining slopes stand trees of the growth of years, which have been spared to adorn the grounds of the palace. The terrace on the north west side, which is 1,000 ft. long and 160 ft. wide, supported by Italian arcades, will cover the railway station, from which access will be had to the building directly at the ends of the three transepts, and to which station all the railway companies of London will ultimately have

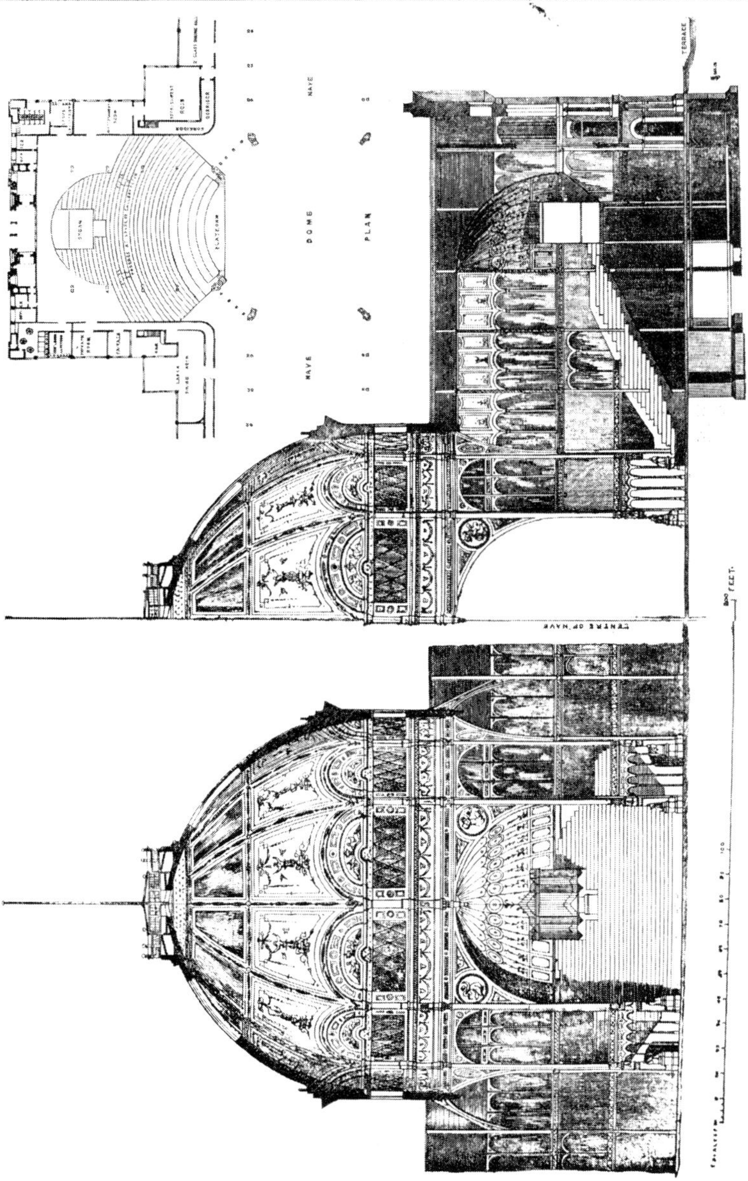

THE ALEXANDRA PALACE, MUSWELL HILL.—SECTION THROUGH DOME.

THE ALEXANDRA PALACE, MUSWELL HILL.

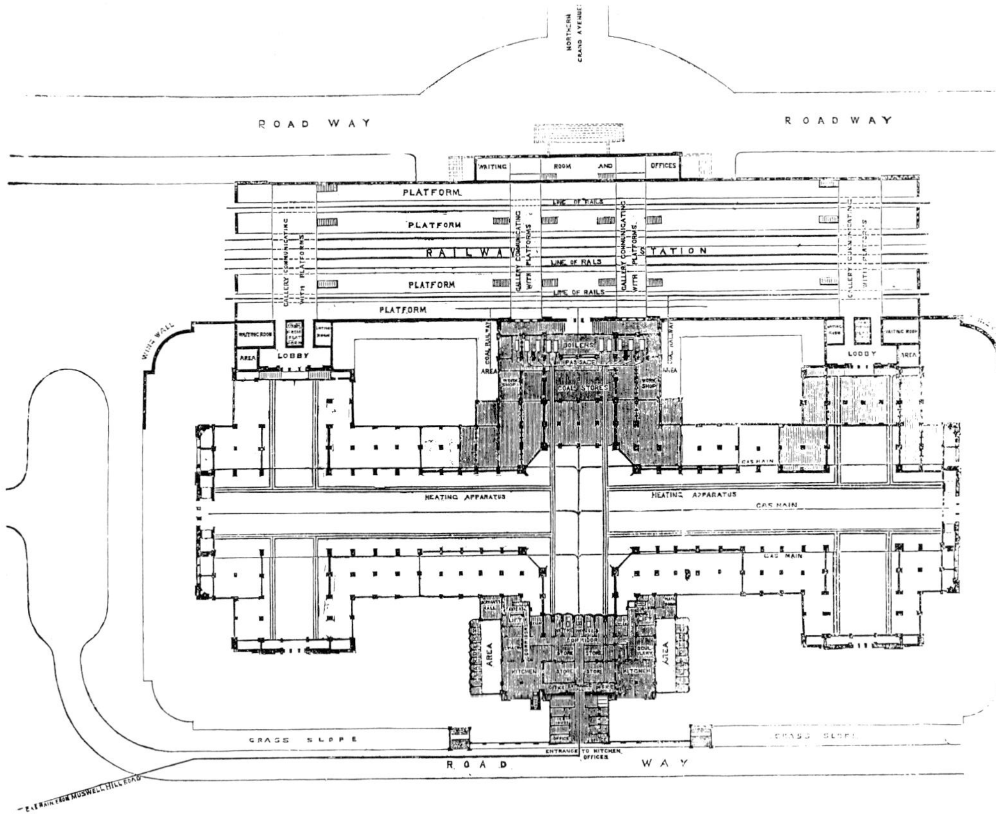

PLAN OF BASEMENT.

trains running for the convenience of visitors to the palace. There will be a covered carriage entrance which will form, at the same time, a conservatory at the end of the nave, communicating by an easy drive with the public road.'

'The ground floor on the south east side will be almost entirely devoted to refreshment and dining rooms of various dimensions and classes. These rooms are all provided with french windows, which open on to a verandah overlooking the terrace and sunny slope of the deer park beyond. The basement storey is replete with accommodation in the way of kitchens, scullery, cellars, etc. The student can also spend an instructive day in visiting the picture galleries, museums, library and reading rooms which have been provided, and the ladies' coffee room will be, we are told, a 'perfect paradise."

'The water supply is, of course, the first of the requirements to be attended to, and will be from the New River Company, from whose reservoirs the building is at present supplied by means of a small steam engine of about seven horse power, which pumps the water up to a temporary wooden tank at the level of the gallery. The main from this engine is 6 in. in diameter and is laid in such a manner that it will serve for a permanent supply pipe, should the Palace Company continue to take their water from the New River reservoir. From this tank a 4 in. service main is laid through the centre of the building which, with a little modification, will serve as one of the four mains for the permanent service to the eight large tanks that are to be fixed within the building at a height of 50 ft. from the ground floor. These tanks will contain about 15,000 cubic feet of water, equal to 100,000 gallons which will be sufficient for the service of lavatories and for the domestic purposes of the establishment, and if kept full, for an immediate resource in case of fire. But if it is intended hereafter to form an additional and larger store of water at the building level to be available for such an emergency, this may be readily done on the south terrace. The present steam power will fill the eight tanks in about three hours, so that the day's supply or consumption might, if required, amount to 70,000 or 80,000 gallons. Should it be desirable to erect any fountains requiring a large supply of water it is quite practicable to establish a small engine for the purpose of returning the water, but for the present fountains will not be erected.'

'The lighting of the palace next presents itself as a consideration. The first question naturally is from whence the supply comes. We may assume that the existing gas companies can supply enough, and as the Hornsey gasworks already have a main pipe laid in the Muswell-hill-road, the terms can be easily arranged, so that the Palace Company shall have a supply main equal to their greatest requirements brought to the boundary of their estate, and security for a sufficient supply of gas at a fair and moderate price. This will be more advantageous than any scheme for an independent gasworks, and will be free from the objection that attaches to the erection of gasworks so close to the palace, which would deteriorate the value of the grond for building purposes, however carefully the gasworks might be constructed and managed.' (Extracts from 'The Builder')

From the outset the Palace itself was dogged by difficulties of many kinds. The terrain itself caused problems with subsidence being present and, as one of the contractors put it: 'the hills slipping about like anything' during one winter. This was partly true, as the hills are in part a twenty foot deep gravel bed resting on a soapy clay mass which could become mobile after saturation by heavy rains. On one night some 3–4 acres near the Palace moved several feet, and at another place a 3 inch forward movement was recorded. However, the foundation of the huge building was well anchored and nothing untoward happened, though worry over this and financial ramifications caused great delay in opening. The building was virtually ready to open in 1866, but did not in fact welcome its public until 24th. May 1873. The opening ceremony did not attract Royalty as might have been expected but was performed by the Lord Mayor of London and included a fine concert under the baton of Sir Michael Costa in which the best singers of the period could be heard.

The Palace was visited by 124,124 people in the first fortnight of its existence before tragedy struck.

Railway Contenders

Before the construction of the railway line to Alexandra Palace is described, the pattern of growth of the railway nearby should first be considered. By 1864, just over a decade after the opening of the main line, the Great Northern Railway Company was beginning to experience acute embarrassment at the congestion caused by the bottleneck of tunnels approaching King's Cross. The Midland Railway who were using G.N. metals to gain access to London from Bedford via Hitchin found that they were suffering great delays. The dormitory areas of Greater London were being filled, with hosts of little houses lining the railways and with more affluent villas adorning the available hillsides. On 1st. July 1861 a station had been opened at Seven Sisters Road, a modest effort of two wooden platforms next to the Hornsey Wood Tea Gardens. In 1869 the Gardens, for some good reason known only to the local authority, were renamed Finsbury Park and of course the station name followed accordingly.

This starting point was chosen by a small company with a long name, the Edgware, Highgate and London Railway, to build a line out to Edgware through Highgate. This would be 8¾ miles and powers were obtained for its construction on 3rd. June 1862. It seems logical nowadays that such a line should be considered, but at the time it must have been fired by some pioneering spirit as the area was very rural indeed through Highgate and Finchley, ending up at little Edgware with a population of 705! The Great Northern had beamed in an avuncular way on the enterprise, had sponsored it and then swallowed it up one month before it opened 22nd. August 1867. The line ran from the Edgware Branch signal cabin, (the Up line flying over the main lines) was double with heavy earthworks on grades of up to 1 in 59 to Highgate. Initially the line was single from Highgate to Edgware, the double track being extended to Finchley Central by 1870.

The EHLR was a vigorous infant with quite ambitious ideas, the principal being of course the main run from Seven Sisters Road to Highgate, costing £96,000, of which the GNR subscribed one third, and a proposal for 1¾ mile long link with the nearby Tottenham and Hampstead Joint, which was not built.

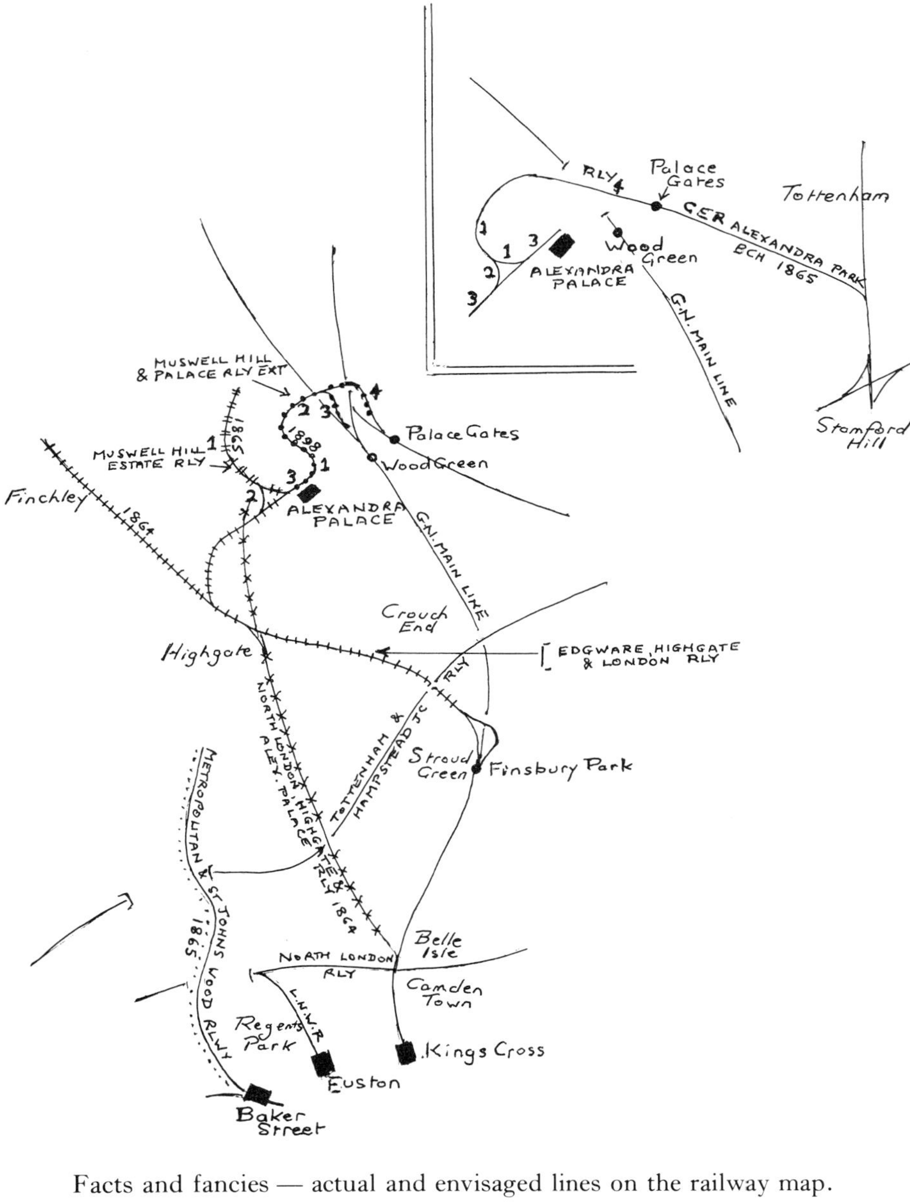

Facts and fancies — actual and envisaged lines on the railway map.

It is true that the EHLR had ideas for circling the Palace and running down to the main line at Wood Green, thus creating a continuous reverse loop. This fact has never been made clear by fellow historians who have always assumed that the Great Eastern Palace Gates station was the only goal. In a letter dated 9th January 1864 the Chairman of the GNR suggested the possibility of such a railway and that it could be laid on the surface, 'like those at Balaclava' with a gradient of 1 in 70 or thereabouts to this 'Leipsic Fair', The cost would be about £9,000. This suggestion was raised again on 23rd. July and on 17th. August 1864 a conference took place between the representatives of the Edgware Company and the GNR to discuss the circular railway. One rather amusing comment recorded came from the EHLR who protested that people would only pass one way over their line if it were part of a loop, with consequent loss of revenue.

Another interesting variation on the theme was embodied in the Muswell Hill Estate Company's Railway, the Bill for which was deposited in December 1865. This used the same arc running northwards and round westwards from the site of the palace to the estate boundary which lay hard by Wood Green GN tunnel. This was Railway No. 1, Nos. 2 and 3 being the sides of the triangle within the estate linking the EHLR branch to the Palace terminus.

Eyes were now turned to the Palace site, and in 1864 the EHLR obtained powers for a line of 1 mile 11 chains from Highgate station to Muswell Hill at the boundary of the park. In December 1864 the North London, Highgate and Alexandra Park Railway put forward a strong proposal to reach the site of the new pleasure grounds. A Railway No. 1 was to commence in the Parish of St. Mary Islington at a junction with the North London Railway west of the bridge over Caledonian Road and terminating at Highgate Hill west of the Highgate Archway Company's land, with an extension to the northern side of the proposed palace at Muswell Hill. A connection would also be made to the EHLR at Highgate, and the intention of the Company was 'to make effectual provision for the speedy, direct and convenient interchange, transmission and delivery of traffic between, from, to, at and over the railways and stations of the above line, the London, Watford and Edgware Junction and North London Railway Companies.' Generous terms were also offered for the interchange of the former Companies' staff, the mutual servicing of engines and rolling stock and the sharing of tolls. One other intention of the Company was to take over the Highgate Archway Company, lift their system of tolls and turn the thoroughfare into a public highway, perhaps a rather unusual act towards a potential competitor.

This promising consortium was opposed by the Great Northern who pointed out quite rightly that theirs would be the more direct and preferred route.

The Metropolitan and Metropolitan District Railways were of course in operation by this time, and in 1864 they proposed a line from Swiss Cottage to Hampstead, with a possible extension to Highgate and Alexandra Palace. This would have put a scar across the unspoiled Heath, so was doomed because of its unpopularity.

In December 1865 the Great Eastern Railway deposited a Bill in Parliament for its own Alexandra Palace branch which was envisaged, surprisingly enough, as commencing south of the park at a triangular junction with the EHLR, Railways 2 and 3, and extended by Railway No. 1 from the north east corner of the palace for 550 yd. to the north. This line made quite a wide arc which was transformed into a semicircle by Railway No. 4 which passed eastwards over Wood Green tunnel and south east to the village of West Green and terminating on the Seven Sisters Road 300 yd. north of its junction with the London-Tottenham road, connecting there with the Great Eastern line from Bethnal Green to Broxbourne Jc. and the Tottenham and Hampstead Joint line. A later proposal brought the ambitious Great Eastern branch to the GNR Wood Green station at Palace Gates, which was constructed for through running but not used as such for passenger purposes.

Construction of the branch from Highgate to Muswell Hill station at the boundary of the park was leisurely, and the land was purchased in 1867 from the Muswell Hill Estate Company. In that year an agreement was reached on 29th. October, in which the following was stipulated:

1 The Alexandra Palace Company to make a station under the terrace of the Palace for passengers with all the necessary platforms, bridges, steps, approaches and conveniences and the necessary waiting rooms, booking offices and all the usual and necessary conveniences for the extent of traffic which may have to be worked to and from the station, and to keep it lighted when needed and at all times in thorough and proper repair and cleanliness.
2 The Great Northern Company to complete the Edgware and Highgate Railway's Muswell Hill branch to the boundary of the premises of the Park with two lines of rails.
3 The Alexandra Palace Company to construct the extension of the Railway from the boundary of the Park into the station as a double line of rails and three platforms running the whole length of the terrace, connected at the end by a turntable and with one or two lines at the West end for a spare engine, and connections, crossings and signals to be shown.
4 The Great Northern Railway to have the use, in perpetuity, of the station, and as long as they have the right to sole access, they will work the railway.
5 If any other company should have permission to use the line, the branch and station shall be in the control of the Great Northern.
6 Any other company joining the said line shall find its own accom-

Rural Calm at Muswell Hill.

Muswell Hill Platforms.

Cabin in the Clearing, Crouch End.

Waiting for arrivals — Muswell Hill exterior.

modation inside the Park and north of the Great Northern accommodation.

7 The Great Northern Company to provide staff.

8 The Great Northern Company to work the traffic efficiently and to issue tickets including admission from every station south of Wood Green including the London, Chatham and Dover Company stations and Metropolitan.

The Great Northern Railway shall, from time to time, issue tickets including admission from stations north of Wood Green.

10 Day tickets shall be interchangable between either Muswell Hill and Wood Green.

Construction of the line began in 1871, and at about the same time the Muswell Hill Estate Company caused work to begin on their little extension within the Park from Muswell Hill to the terminus. Tenders for this had been submitted on 17th. December 1867 and the amounts and variations are quite remarkable. They include the station itself.

Pickering: £48,914 11s. 6d. Ritson: £44,579. Humphreys: £27,675.
Firbank: £38,975. Nowell: £40,000. Mansfield-Price: £40,974.
Harrison-Hodgson: £47,697. Macleman: £40,887. Wainwright: £34,500.
Nelson: £52,920 13s. 4d. Relf: £47,800.

Mr. Humphreys obviously had something to learn about estimates, or perhaps it was all the others who were out of step? Mr. Nowell had obviously settled for a nice round figure, opposed to Mr. Nelson who was meticulous. In the event the last tender was chosen.

The Palace with its grounds of 480 acres covering a larger area than Hyde Park opened on 24th. May 1873 with a concert, a flower show, archery contest and £1,000 given away as prizes. The combined branches were ready for the traffic, in fact the Palace section had been prepared since the previous summer. The Muswell Hill Company owned no rolling stock except for a rumoured locomotive and, as stated above, everything was controlled and operated by the GNR. Entry to the Palace was free for a time, though the rail fare was charged. Inside the grounds there was an inner charge of 2/6 or 5/- on some days.

On the opening day the Directors of the Alexandra Palace Company, that is Lord Fermough (Chairman), Mr. Lightley-Simpson (Deputy), The Hon. C. Vivian and Messrs. Elliot and Martin left King's Cross at 12.25 p.m. to view the grounds and sample the running. No doubt they had shown great interest in the fare scales for passengers, as the Company took shares in the receipts:

12½% of all receipts at Wood Green station.

25% on all tickets booked to the Palace from north of Wood Green station.

They had also insisted that the fare to Muswell Hill should be the same as that to Wood Green, and that to Alexandra Palace no more than an extra penny than Wood Green.

Opening day return fares from King's Cross including admission were:

1st.	2nd.	3rd
2/5d.	2/2d.	1/9d.

with the following applying along the route, excluding admission:

	Single			Return		
	1st.	2nd.	3rd.	1st.	2nd.	3rd.
City Stations	1/2d.	10d.	7d.	1/10d.	1/4d.	1/-
King's Cross	11d.	9d.	6d.	1/5d.	1/2d.	9d.
Holloway	8d.	6d.	4d.	1/1d.	1/-	6d.
Finsbury Park	7d.	5d.	3½d.	11d.	8d.	5d.
Crouch End	7d.	5d.	3½d.	10d.	7d.	5d.
Highgate	5d.	4d.	2½d.	8d.	6d.	5d.

On the Whit Monday over 60,000 passengers were carried, and the number present exceeded those at Crystal Palace on that day. Then, on Monday 9th. June 1873 tragedy struck.

Disaster!

On that day between noon and two o'clock the Palace was destroyed by fire, leaving a blackened ruin with everything razed to the ground except for the gable ends and parts of the walls. The 'Illustrated London News' reported:

'The cause of the fire was the carelessness of workmen employed to repair the leadwork in the roof of the great dome. A morsel of red hot charcoal, dropped from a brazier, set fire to the timber and papier maché in a crevice where it fell near the upper gallery outside the dome, while the men were gone to dinner at half past twelve. In a few minutes, almost before the alarm could be given, the central part of the dome, inside as well as outside, was involved in flames which quickly spread in every direction till the whole vast building was consumed. The first outbreak within the building was observed by many persons, and shouts of alarm ran through the nave and transepts, while the multitude of visitors escaped as fast as they could by every door. Hydrants abounded in the main passages and galleries, many of these were opened by the attendants, but from the first it was discovered that no force of water was on, and all hope of arresting the progress of the fire was precluded. When the alarm reached the offices of the manager and secretary, the united efforts of their staff were devoted to rescuing from destruction the most valuable objects of art in the palace. The loan collection of modern pictures and drawings was torn down from the gallery walls and carried by files of men out into the park.'

'The alarm of the palace being on fire was telegraphed immediately to the different Metropolitan fire brigade stations and to the King's Cross station of the Great Northern Railway. Mr. Oakley, General Manager of the line, at once sent down the only two fire engines kept at King's Cross, each by special train, to Wood Green, where they arrived almost as soon as the local engine from that village had been got out. Six steam fire engines left London almost simultaneously, under the conduct of the best men in the force. On their arrival the brigade with their engines were speedily in action, and worked from a valley on the western side of the burning building, where, however, there was but an indifferent supply of water. With a large reservoir and the New River at the foot of the hill, there does not seem to have been any

GREATER LONDON COUNCIL

Top: Alexandra Palace, 9th June 1873.
Bottom: Looking across the Station after the Fire.

arrangements for pumping it up in quantities. The firemen's hose, too, had to be carried over a line of railway, and they had to contend with a stiff breeze which greatly fanned the flames.'

'Meantime the fire had spread through every nook and corner of the edifice, travelling downwards from the roof, first along the galleries, then attacking the main body of the nave and transepts, increasing in fury as it came in contact with the more combustible materials of the building, especially the theatre and the great concert hall. The flames spread along the roof which fell in great flakes upon the area below, splitting the floor in places and distributing fire as it descended. At length the cord of the union jack, which had floated from the dome, was burnt through, and the flag itself, coming down with a run, disappeared in the burning ruins.'

'The organ, one of the grandest ever built, which stood on the north side of the centre transept, is destroyed, with its complex fittings. It was built by Willis, under the superintendence of Sir Michael Costa, and had 101 stops, eighty of which were sounding stops, and was worked by two steam engines, one eight horse power and the other thirteen. The fine orchestra in front of the organ, which was sufficiently large to accommodate 1,000 performers, and the front of which was adorned with busts of Beethoven, Handel, Rossini, Verdi, Mendelssohn and Auber, has likewise disappeared, and so has the theatre with its pretty drop-scene, and all the rest of its belongings. The whole of the interior is an unsightly ruin from beginning to end, completely open to the sky, and filled with iron material twisted into all kinds of fantastic shapes, and other rubbish.'

'Captain Shaw reports as follows on the fire: 'Called to a fire at 12.30 p.m. by the police and strangers at Muswell Hill, North, the Alexandra Palace Company (Ltd). Supposed cause of fire — plumbers at work on the roof. Contents unknown. Building insured in the Mercantile and Phoenix Fire Offices. Six of Messrs. Shand and Mason's land steamers and three manual engines at work. The fire was extinguished by the firemen and strangers; and the water was supplied by the New River Company. A brick building about 900 ft. by 400 ft. burnt out and roof off."

'It is deeply to be regretted that, notwithstanding every effort made by the directors to effect adequate insurance against fire upon the building, it had been found impossible to insure for more than £150,000 — a small portion of the cost of the palace and its contents. The loss to the individual exhibitors and others will be very great, and hundreds of persons are thrown out of employment. Much sympathy is felt on their account, especially for the poor women who had hired stalls in the bazaar and whose goods are destroyed. A subscription for their relief is proposed. Two persons lost their lives in the fire. One was an elderly man named Charles Casey, employed to take care of the plate belonging to Messrs. Bertram and Roberts, the contractors for refreshments. He was found dead in the plate room, a large fireproof chamber, which during the fire had been surrounded by flames. Another man, Alfred Lloyd, had escaped from this room with difficulty; but Casey remained, and was either suffocated or died of apoplexy. The store of plate was saved by their joint efforts. A night watchman named Jordan, is also said to have perished. Several of the firemen were severely injured, and are in the Great Northern Hospital.'

The Great Northern Railway were successful in saving from the many sparks and falling embers their own property at the station, which was mainly of wood. Trains were run frequently so that sight-seers could get a close glimpse of the ruins which, if anything, looked even more imposing than the pristine building had done.

The proprietors were not unduly daunted by their misfortune. During the week following the disaster they made successful efforts to draw the crowds to the palace site, pointing out that much remained to be enjoyed in the fine summer weather. Many thousands came to see the display of rhododendrons, cricket matches, archery and a balloon ascent by Mr. Coxwell. Perhaps most surprising and enterprising was the firework display put on one evening a fortnight after the blaze, with set pieces in the ruins re-enacting the burning of the building. For the unfortunate stall-holders a subscription was collected at these events, while the Crystal Palace Company generously donated the whole of one Monday's takings to help the relief of those most afflicted. One of the foremen employed on the site, Thomas Larner, died later as a result of being struck by a portion of the great dome, bringing the total of fatalities to four.

On 18th June, Henry Oakley, Chairman of the Great Northern, wrote to each of his directors as follows:

"The Board is of course aware of the destruction of the Alexandra Palace by fire on Monday, the 9th. Inst. Practically the whole building was consumed in a very short time. We certainly intend to continue the trains to the Alexandra Park (sic) station. We ceased running trains to the Alexandra Park branch during last week, and carried all the people who wished to see the ruins to Wood Green only."

At the urgent request of the Manager of the Alexandra Palace Company who desired to utilise the place for outdoor amusement as much as possible, we have resumed running a moderate service, the results of which we shall watch.

The destruction of the Palace is indeed a piece of misfortune, as it practically renders useless the Alexandra Park branch, at any rate for the time that the building is in the course of re-erection.

I have seen Messrs. Kelk and Lucas and I have from them that, including the freehold, about a million of money has been spent. They will be unable to replace the building for the amount of which it was insured, or indeed anything like it, and they are now considering how the balance of funds shall be raised.

Capital: £450,000 Mortgage Debentures.
£200,000 Preferential Shares.
£350,000 Ordinary Shares.

Building insured for £120,000 (Less than the amount mentioned above.) It would cost a further £200,000 to restore and furnish it.

Looking at the success of the undertaking and the urgency of finding further capital to restore it, Kelk and Lucas suggest that probably you might be willing to purchase the line and station from the end of your own line to the palace and thus secure for yourselves the poll tax of 1d. per head which they were to receive for providing it.

The station and their piece of land excluding the line cost, they tell me, about £70,000, this of course being largely caused by the erection of the terrace over the station in connection with the Palace.

I told Kelk and Lucas that I sincerely regretted the destruction of their building and the loss which it entailed on them, but that I could only submit the suggestion that they have thrown out for your consideration.'

Already, then, the line was in trouble with dark, hints for its closure disguised in a shift of responsibility for its operation and a modification of its services which were reduced from 18 to 7 trains each way soon after the fire. The trouble was that there was, as yet, little other traffic on Muswell Hill apart from the Park itself, and the few villas which did exist found the stations at Wood Green and Highgate within handy reach of their own gigs and traps.

A more direct approach was made to the Manager of the Alexandra Palace Company by the Superintendent of the line on 3rd. July 1873, as follows:

Gilbert R. Redgrave.

Dear Sir,

I called at your office yesterday but you were out. It was to tell you that my anticipations as to the traffic to the Palace station have, I regret to say, not been fully realised. The traffic is now less than I anticipated and I find that it does not average more than five persons per train. This does not of course cover even the cost of the engine, leaving out altogether carriage staff, etc., and in fact the whole of the Palace branch service of trains is now being carried on at a very serious loss.

We have had several fetes advertised to be held in the present month. We shall not object, therefore, to continue the service to the end of July, but I shall be obliged to report the result of the present working to my Directors, and I think your Directors will be of the opinion that we should not run the branch trains after July. Will you be so good as to mention this to them at your first meeting, and let me known the result?

It is quite evident that the traffic has now concentrated at Wood Green, and this will be the case as long as the attractions are in the neighbourhood of the Race Course, for which Wood Green offers better accommodation than does the Palace station. We can increase the service from this station if necessary. My advice would be to close the Alexandra Palace branch after the present month.

Yours faithfully,
Frances P. Cockshott.

This was in fact done on the last day of the month, and the only regular movement was a daily pickup goods train out to Muswell Hill yard and back.

During this period the Railway Company was also involved in litigation concerning 'The Green Man' public house at Muswell Hill whose landlord complained of slipping of the soil towards the cutting which was slowly taking with it his coach house, stables and a portion of the garden wall.

The Phoenix Arises

Work had soon begun on the second Alexandra Palace, with the first bricks laid on 10th. October 1873. 'The Builder' magazine for 15th. August of that year reported as follows:

'The new building stands on the same spot as the old one did, and is of the same length and breadth, but the enclosed area is much larger, it covering 7½ acres, for while the first may be described as long and comparatively narrow, with a nave intersected by three transepts projecting considerably at both facades, the second building is a complete parallelogram.'

'As in the old building, the great hall forms the central transept, but in place of a dome it has a semicircular and very lofty roof supported on four rows of columns, and thus a grand hall is obtained 386 ft. long by 184 ft. wide, with parallel sides, in which is a series of doors, and when necessary it can be shut off entirely from the rest of the building.'

'Right and left of the great hall are two courts, one of which is roofed with glass, and the other open to the air; these enclosed gardens are each 120 ft. long and 140 ft. wide. On each side of these courts are corridors of the same length, those on one side being for picture galleries, and those on the other to be decorated with sculpture, objects of art, and flowers.'

'At the north end of the great hall is the grand orchestra, seating 1,150 performers, with organ by Willis.'

'On the top of the four towers are water reservoirs containing 16,000 gallons each, and at the angles of the central hall are four other reservoirs of 7,000 gallons each, the whole supplied by steam pumps from the New River Company's reservoirs. Completely surrounded by its own park the building is accessible on every side, and the railway being carried beneath the terrace, stairs on each side of the great hall lead from the platform of the station into the palace. The company's board room, and the offices of the managers, clerks and assistants are on the two floors on each side of the eastern entrance. A post and telegraph office will be formed to the left of the south entrance, and a covered carriageway at the eastern entrance.

The materials used for the facades of the building are white Huntingdon and dark coloured yellow bricks, the mouldings and ornaments being of

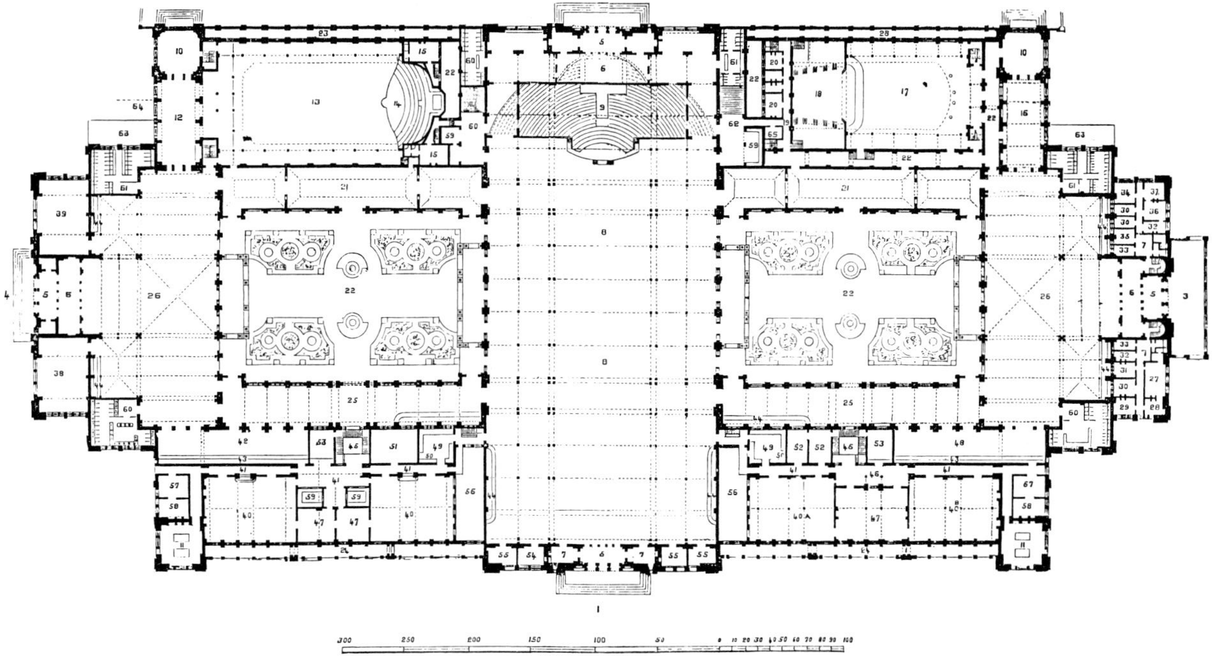

THE NEW ALEXANDRA PALACE.——*Plan.*

1. South terrace.
2. North terrace.
3. East (inclosed carriage) entrance.
4. West entrance.
5. Outside lobby.
6. Inside lobby.
7. Lobby.
8. Great central hall, 386 ft. by 184 ft. 6 in.
9. Great orchestra: organ over inside lobby.
10. Tower.
11. Billiard-room.
12. Concert-room corridor.
13. Concert-room, 145 ft. by 95 ft. 7 in.
14. Orchestra.
15. Artists' room.
16. Theatre corridor.
17. Theatre, 104 ft. 6 in. by 83 ft. 6 in.
18. Stage, 52 ft. deep.
19. Artists' entrance.
20. Artists' retiring-rooms.
21. Exhibition gallery, 30 ft. wide each.
22. Open court.
23. Open area.
24. Open colonnade.
25. Glazed corridor, 30 ft. wide each.
26. Conservatory, 201 ft. by 104 ft. 4 in. each.
27. Board-room.
28. Secretary's office.
29. Secretary's clerks.
30. Clerks' office.
31. Board's refreshment-room.
32. Waiting-room.
33. Porter.
34. First superintendent.
35. Second superintendent.
36. Manager's room.
37. Manager's clerks.
38. Library and reading-room, 60 ft. by 40 ft.
39. Theatre for special purposes, 60 ft. by 40 ft.
40. First-class banquet-room, 73 ft. by 50 ft. and 67 ft. by 50 ft.
40*a*. First-class coffee-room, 67 ft. by 50 ft.
40*b*. Grille and cold meats room, 70 ft. by 50 ft.
41. Serving passage.
42. Refreshment-bar.
43. Buffet.
44. Refreshment-buffet.
45. Entrance.
46. Vestibule.
47. Anteroom.
48. Tea and coffee bar.
49. Serving-room.
50. Lift.
51. Staff-room.
52. Messrs. Bertram and Roberts' offices.
53. Wine-bar.
54. Telegraph and post-office.
55. Office.
56. Glazed court.
57. Wash-up.
58. Glass.
59. Hats, coats, &c.
60. Ladies' retiring-room.
61. Gentlemen's retiring-room.
62. From railway platform.
63. Gateway incline.
64. Corridor to proposed aquarium.
65. Stores.

Portland cement. The corner towers are surmounted with decorated mansard roofs and metal finials and are 180 ft. high from the ground floor. The extreme length of the new palace is 897 ft. 6 in. and it is 386 ft. wide.'

'For those who rejoice in statistics we are able to record that 15,000,000 bricks have been used, and 3,000 tons of lime. The wrought iron, 764 tons, was supplied by Messrs. Handyside of Derby; the cast iron, 1,354 tons by the Staveley Works, Staffordshire.'

When the new place was opened on May Day 1875 the full train service was restored to accommodate some 21,000 who attended on that day.

The programme of events offered to the public during August 1875 might be considered as typical, with a Special Entertainment for the Bank Holiday (2nd.) and both an orchestra and a military band operating in the Grove on most days. On 17th. and 18th. were two days of horse racing, while on 24th. and 25th. a Flower Show was held. On Monday 23rd. was a Great Fete of Railway Officials and Servants, with general attractions. On each Sunday the park was open to season ticket holders only, who were rewarded for their interest in the success of the palace by being given the exclusive rights to promenade in the grounds and to inspect the galleries on these special occasions. Free access was also granted to the Company's Reading Room, while the Writing Room could be used for a nominal charge. Additionally, 20% of all receipts from season tickets of one guinea each was invested in the purchase of paintings and works of art for the galleries, while ticket holders could enter a competition held yearly in May to acquire a work of art, thus stimulating Victorian culture and the flourishing arts industry.

General admission to the palace and park was one shilling and was to remain the same for very many years. On the first Saturday of each month, however, the admission was increased to 2/6d., while on three days a year seasons were not usable and a special admission rate was charged for all.

Whit Monday 1875, when 94,000 attended, proved to be a memorable one for a writer to one of the local newspapers, who was 'one of the unfortunates who had the evil inspiration to go a-pleasuring to Muswell Hill on a very promising forenoon.' He started in the forenoon, but the sun had long been in the decline before he reached his destination. He took a first class return through ticket at Victoria which was to frank him on to the Great Northern line at King's Cross. He thought himself lucky to get a seat in the guard's van of the second train that arrived from the stuffy underground passage, and what a misery that devious passage in the dark is on a broiling day. 'After calling at some half a score of stations, at all of which masses of holiday folk were waiting, we drew at last at King's Cross, jumped out and rushed upwards into the open air which was very grateful (sic) although the sun did daze, across to the GN terminus. Thousands of people who had purchased tickets which purported to convey them somewhere were sweltering on the space between two lines of rails, wedged together like so many sheep in a pen, swaying, pushing, perspiring, irritated beyond measure at seeing their prized holiday wasted away. At infrequent intervals a long line of carriages glided to the platform, and then there was a fierce rush and scream of weak women.'

'How to get home? Multiply the morning crowds by ten and the tussles troubles and pestilential annoyance of disappointments repeated over and over again.

There was a block at the Palace station and a block at Wood Green station, and not a trap to be had for love or money on the outside.'.

The writer concludes this floridly written tale of woe by describing how he got into a compartment with 14 others, among whom was a clergyman who tried to convert all of them. This gentleman had very opportunity as the journey home lasted from 8.45 p.m. to 1.20 a.m. along the shortened route of 4½ miles to Holloway only, where everyone was decanted as a light engine had become derailed in Copenhagen tunnel.

Mr Williams' party of Ragged School Union teachers was not among the early visitors. He had written to the Great Northern Railway on 6th. May 1876 asking for a quotation for a day's outing for 200 of his paid teachers in the City area and hoped to travel from Moorgate. Mr. Cockshott wrote back at once to say that Mr. Williams would only be able to enjoy a concession fare if his party numbered at least 250. Back came the tart reply from Mr. Williams on the 7th. June that the GNR were in no way as liberal as the London, Chatham and Dover Company who readily gave reductions for parties of 100 and included admission to Crystal Palace (the Alexandra Palace admission had been quoted at 8d. per head); thus he was taking his business elsewhere. He also wrote a letter to the Alexandra Palace Company couched in the same terms. They, in turn, wrote to the GNR and asked if they could really afford to discourage traffic of that kind, enclosing the tariff for party rates to Crystal Palace and including admission.:

London Bridge, Victoria or Ludgate Hill to Crystal Palace.

Parties of	100–250	1/4d.
	250–500	1/3d.
	500–750	1/2d.
	750–1000	1/1d.
	1000+	1/-

The Great Northern would not give way, but simply quoted their own charges for parties of 250–1000, excluding admission:

from King's Cross 1/4d.
Moorgate, Ludgate Hill and Broad St. 1/6d.

The North London Railway was now running quite a smart service of trains to the Palace from Broad Street with the GNR's somewhat grudging consent.

The GNR was acutely embarrassed by the congestion developing on its main route to and from the north, and no doubt it often cursed the Alexandra Palace traffic from an operational, if not from a financial point of view. We have mentioned the inauguration of the North London trains to and from Broad Street. These had a path made easier for them by the construction of the spur of 1872 from Finsbury Park to Canonbury which enabled freights to avoid Copenhagen tunnel. In the event this was no advantage, as it was found more convenient to reach the new Farringdon Street goods depot by running direct. Having the new link, the GNR naturally wished to obtain running powers to Broad Street. These were refused by the North London line who had the big and influential London and North Western breathing down their necks and who would not countenance such bravado. The GNR offered the NLR running powers over their lines to several suburban termini including Alexandra Palace and High Barnet, but they were the losers here, as no reciprocal running powers were to be awarded them, thus, their lines grew even busier, with over 70 NLR Up trains by 1906, reduced services continuing well into British Rail days though worked by the London & North Eastern Rly after the Hitler war.

To ease ticket collection at King's Cross, Holloway station had been opened at which all local trains called for inspection. This of course tended to cause further hold-ups as irritated commuters were persuaded to part with their tickets. The main troubles were, however, caused by the tunnels which at times accounted for delays of half an hour or more on the last mile or so into the terminus. King's Cross was always a badly planned station to operate until the recent track realignment.

Work was authorised for a second bore for Copenhagen tunnel in 1866, which was completed on the west side for goods traffic in 1877. Likewise Gasworks tunnel was doubled, a second bore for two Up tracks coming into use on 4th. Mach 1878.

Still the flow of commuters, like Topsy, grew and grew, and third bores were opened for Copenhagen in June 1886, double line Up side, and for Gasworks in June 1892 on the Down side.

The hub of much of the suburban activity was Finsbury Park station, which had grown from two to four platforms from 14th. December 1874 and which was, in many ways, ahead of its time with its flying junction at the north end carrying the Up Highgate line and burrowing junction at the other end taking the Down North London and Great Northern goods traffic from Canonbury. Much of the goods traffic had to be resorted here, so that there were extensive yards hereabouts, such as the Ferme Park yards opened in 1888.

By 1912 there were up to 550 trains each day calling at the same platforms, with six running lines through the station. Platforms 9 and 10 and an extra running line were added in 1911. Each of the local lines had a platform face on each side of it, and in its heyday at peak periods traffic was arranged so that three suburban trains might stand in the station side by side and passengers, if they found it convenient, could pass through the compartments to gain other platforms or different trains. By carefully scheduling main line traffic the main, slow and branch lines could be used for this purpose. Observers have noted typical simultaneous departures at 8.19 a.m. of trains for King's Cross, Moorgate and Broad Street, with an equivalent at 6.25 p.m. for Enfield (ex Broad St.) Wood Green and semi-fast to Hitchin.

The chequered career of the new Alexandra Palace continued, this time with its closure in 1876 and with it the branch line. Things were becoming commercially very difficult for the Alexandra Palace Company, and in March 1877 the Palace and grounds were offered for sale by auction through Messrs. Norton, Trist and Watney under an order in liquidation. A huge crowd was present at the sale rooms in London, and the reserve price of £800,000 was not reached by offers which only touched £445,000. Private offers were invited for the property, which came into the hands of the London Financial Association at a total price of £408,000, this including 16 acres of freehold building land for £16,000 and the Park and Palace for £390,000. Included were 'the whole of the chattels, and such things as the organ, statues and other fixtures and fittings about the place.' The purchase was considered an astute one, as the land available was valued at £700 per acre which meant, in toto, that the Palace and Park had in fact been purchased for a little over £200,000! To add some other final figures of interest, the banqueting hall cost £12,000, the circus and the grandstand £10,000 each.

Both the London Financial Association and the shareholders of the Muswell Hill Estate Company gave their approval to the sale of lots of the Alexandra Palace land for building purposes, this being agreed in April 1877.

The Palace and grounds opened again for the season of 1878 and of course the railway recommenced its train service, carrying half a million during that year, as a result of which the Muswell Hill Estate Company was able to pay a 3% dividend to its shareholders.

The books of the Muswell Hill Estate Company had always been kept in a healthy state and showed a credit balance, even though it was not always a hearty one. To Messrs. Kelk and Lucas went a handsome £3,192 in 1872, as a final payment on the construction, along with £507 to the Great Northern. Then, the first financial quarter to December 1873 brought in £21 in traffic and tolls, the income rising to a maximum of £4656 for the first half year of 1881, to top up a healthy balance of £1939 for the previous half year. Sir John Kelk and Mr. C.T. Lucas came out of matters well, each receiving half yearly interest on £1650 Lloyd's bonds at 4%, and some late dividends on shares in the London Financial Association on £35,000 stock at 7%. Each received £605 at the second half year in 1876, and these payments continued until 1885, when the yield was only £48. The damage caused by the fire necessitated the expenditure of £99 on 7th. October 1875 for sundry works to the station booking office and gates, while on 23rd. October 1877 Mr. Pocock received £86 for works done at the station. On 2nd. October 1876 the Royal Assurance Co. was paid £62. 10s. for fire coverage, while on 15th. January 1878 the sum of £5 was given as a gratuity to the Fire Brigade, no doubt with the late disaster very much in mind.

Fortunes of pleasure enterprises are so fickle, dependent as they are on the weather and tastes of the day, that in spite of such healthy returns at the outset, the park and its huge building lost popularity, and its owners, the London Financial Association, began to fail. In the very prosperous year of 1878 some 80 acres north of the site were sold off for housing, and it was reported that the whole site of 240 acres was due to go the same way. The new housing did go some way towards helping railway receipts; the little branch now had another raison d'être and could keep solvent from the growing band of commuters settling on Muswell Hill. However, these were apparently insufficient to prevent closure of the line during protracted periods when the Palace was 'resting', as between August 1882 and March 1885, and twice more from September 1885 to March 1889 and a long period from August 1889 to August 1898. However, the Race Course was in regular use and served from Wood Green. Staff on the branch must have had a rough time wondering how secure their employment was, although there were times when the line was in use in spite of the Palace closure, as from March 1891 to April 1892.

At a meeting of the Muswell Hill Estates Co. on 11th. February 1885, the Secretary stated that, prior to the line being reopened for traffic, certain repairs and renewals were necessary. He had been in communication with Mr. Oakley of the GNR who, on 19th. January, had written and enclosed an estimate of works necessary which amounted to £1,077. This he submitted to his Chairman and to Messrs. Lucas Bros. Mr. Oakley was asked to put the work in hand at once. Neglect and the elements, had caused further deterioration of the property, and on 24th. March 1887 the GNR announced their willingness to repair Muswell Hill and Alexandra Palace stations for £400–500 if they could be released from the passenger toll. No progress was apparently forthcoming in this direction, as Mr. Oakley again wrote asking if one halfpenny per head could be charged instead of one penny. The 'new' station at Alexandra Palace was completed and opened by Mr. Oakley on 1st. November 1889, just in time for a special fireworks event in the park. The total repair bill was below the amount of the tender, at £224 13s. 6d. However, Mr. Adams, a local builder, was asked to provide a new approach road to Alexandra Palace station at a sum of £2,798 15s.

During this turbulent period the Muswell Hill Railway became the Muswell Hill and Palace Railway, and in 1897 its owners made a bid to revive the original idea of connecting with the GN and GE lines down at Wood Green. Earlier, the GN themselves had hinted at something similar and in a letter to Henry Oakley dated 16th. February 1885 referring to this proposal Mr. Frederick Propert, Secretary of the Estates Board wrote as follows:

'The working of an Electric Railway in connection with the Palace might prove a source of competition and injury to this Company. They cannot agree to the suggestions contained in your letter, but must regret that the terms of working must be those which have been in force whenever the railway was open.'

Electric Traction Arrives

The London Finance Association had reduced the size of the park to about 200 acres and developed housing, but had failed to make anything like a success of the enterprise, hence the fitful opening and closure of the railway. In October 1897 a lease was taken on the property by a Mr. Thomas John Hawkins, a builder who had had some experience of similar matters at a pleasure fair at Wembley Park. He undertook to reopen both the Park and Palace from Easter 1898 and to maintain the shilling admission charge. The railway reopened from 1st. April and at Easter 100,000 visitors were carried by the trains. However, Hawkins looked beyond Wood Green at the growing suburbs to the east and wished to offer easy access for the hordes of potential visitors. He revived a scheme which had first been mooted in 1866 and on several subsequent occasions, namely to extend the Palace Gates line of the Great Eastern up to the Palace itself, and to give some substance to the Great Northern's hinted interest in electric traction. A compromise was reached in the shape of an electric tramway running from the park gates above Wood Green station up to the eastern entrance of the Palace. The ride was to be in part a pleasure one as well as an amenity for those short of breath or stamina, and as the run of line was to be on private land, no Act of Parliament was needed.*

Construction of the 660 yd. standard gauge line began in February 1898, using 60 ft. grooved rails each 85 lb. to the yard. The actual cost of the double line was £11,000. Money could well have been saved using a single track which might have extended the life of this little known line. The track climbed an average gradient of 1 in 13, with two sections of 1 in 11 and 1 in 9. At the upper end was a turning circle of 90 ft. radius on the level, with a short spur running to a shed which housed the four cars. To the rear of the depot was the generating station which contained two 140 lb. steam boilers and 30 hp. engines each driving two dynamos generating 130 amps at 550 volts. The

* In the summer of 1889 Mr Lee Baptry had attempted to set up an overhead cable railway of the ski lift type. However the supports for this collapsed in the early stages of construction, injuring a workman. The whole idea was transferred to an exhibition in Edinburgh later in the same year.

Palace Car bearing Legends of both the County Council and the Owning Company.

Tram climbing towards the Palace.

lower end of the line finished with both lines parallel linked by a trailing crossover for reversal.

The tramway was built by the Berlin firm of Wandruszka Electrical as agents of two parent American firms. The overhead wiring and poles were thus of German type, though the generating gear was British. The four single deck cars which were semi-open were built by the Hamburg tramcar manufacturer Falkenried and seated thirty on cross benches at each end, with twenty more in a central portion open to the elements. Mesh was soon fitted to prevent passengers' hands and heads coming into violent contact with the lineside poles. The ends were glazed to protect the driver. Wheelbase of the cars was 6 ft. and, surprisingly enough, braking was by hand which proved very unreliable on wet days, as on 30th. May 1898 when three passengers were injured during a downhill skid with a full car.

Making mention of the little tramway gives an opportunity to offer more details of the palace routine with which it was essentially linked. Both operated from 10 a.m. to 10.30 p.m. on Mondays to Fridays and to 11 p.m. on Saturdays. At this period the Palace and Park were closed on Sundays. Although the entertainments began at Easter, the tramway was not completed until 13th. May. Nevertheless, until Bonfire Night during the first season, the trams, of which normally two were in operation at a time, carried 172,000 at fares of 2d. up and 1d. down. The round trip took about twelve minutes.

Relations between Hawkins and Wandruszka became strained, the latter seeking mainly to regard the tramway as a shop window where the company's products might be demonstrated, rather than as a serious operation. However, the system opened again for a further season, beginning on 31st. March 1899, and closing with the Palace on 30th. September, this time for good, due in part to the poor weather which had reduced revenue and prevented the operators from covering expenditure. Locally there had been criticism of the differences in fares for each direction, so that 1d. was charged uniformly. The tramway claimed only one victim, a German fitter employed by the company who lost his life in June 1898 due to his own carelessness in alighting from a moving car.

The line was finally removed, apart from the generating station which, perhaps appropriately, became a licensed bar. Had there not been a dispute between the two men most concerned in the existence of the line, and the ultimate bankruptcy of Hawkins, the little route which had run for eighteen months would almost certainly have been taken into the growing local tramway network, as a new line was laid on the same route to the Palace and opened on 11th. April 1906, whilst the MET laid a further line from Turnpike Lane to the West entrance which opened on 6th. December 1905. Both lines had single deck cars and ran only when the park was open.

The sequel to this part of the story is that the Wandruszka Electrical

1570 in L.N.E.R. livery at King's Cross.

Alexandra Palace branch arrival at Finsbury Park.

Company with its tramway collapsed in 1899, and that the four cars survived, going to Cleethorpes and used by the Great Grimsby Street Tramways Company as double deckers, three of them open top. These cars ran until 1926.

Back at Alexandra Palace, the two tram routes to the top of Muswell Hill ran until their replacement by motor vehicles on 23rd. February 1938, firstly from each end, then through the park after the completion of a new road on 28th. May 1938.

However, the story is moving too quickly into the near-present, and it is necessary to journey back to the beginning of the new century.

New Owners and Wartime

As early as 1891 the Chairman of Middlesex Council had proposed the purchase of the Palace and grounds and the Alexandra Palace Trust was formed in February 1901 to provide the highest class of entertainment at the cheapest possible price. It was purchased for the various local authorities mainly through the efforts of Mr. Henry Burt, J.P. The trustees each served for a period of three years — Islington, for instance appointed two, initially Alderman Richard Montford and Mr. S.E. Ramsey, and contributed £14,000 towards the purchase price of £165,000. The other trustees were Middlesex 7, Hornsey 5, Wood Green 5, Tottenham 1, Friern Barnet 1 and Finchley 1. The latter did not contribute financially, though on the other hand Southgate did contribute without having a representative on the board. The Palace now belonged to the people of North London, and every penny spent there went directly or indirectly to the improvement of the public's property.

The Palace was dedicated to the public at a ceremony in the Central Hall, presided over by the Duke of Bedford, Lord Lieutenant of Middlesex. Greeted by a fanfare of Royal Trumpeters, he said that the Palace stood within sight and sound of one of the vastest centres of population the world had ever seen, and had been purchased with the addition of 170 acres of land at less than half the cost of the original buildings. Queen Alexandra herself sent a telegram wishing her namesake 'every success.'

Entertainments abounded, with Fairs (Olde Englishe and Oriental), Military band cncerts in the Grove and something called an Incandescent Bungalow Orchestra of Transparent Splendour, which sounds like a pop group ahead of its time!

Externally the structure was illuminated by the Gulcher Company's largest combined electric light installation in Europe. Within, patrons could sample some of the refreshment prepared with provision for up to 100,000, before going to see the burlesque entitled 'Little Lohengrin' by Mr. F. Bowyer, or perhaps, if this were not to their taste, to assemble to be regaled by Chirgwin the White Eyed Kaffir, Miss Florrie Ford and Atroy, the great Equilibrist. All for a mere shilling, and all from 10 a.m. to 10 p.m.

On 26th. September 1903 30,000 people witnessed Messrs. Pains' firework show which began at 6 p.m. with a daylight display for the younger viewers. As dusk fell the oriental lanterns and fairy lights were switched on along the walks, and Mr. Fulcher's Fairground on the Race Course burst into full illumination. Aquatic fireworks preceded the Great Display at 8.45 p.m., when all visitors were summoned from every part of the ground by maroons to witness possibly the biggest ever display of set pieces which included static representations of public buildings, a 'faery ring' of 150 ft. diameter, Niagara Falls, a Punch and Judy show and an animated tug-of-war.

At about the same time a writer to the "Middlesex Chronicle" complained of the crowds that thronged the area on Sunday afternoons and of the poor service at the tea room set in the subterranean passages of the palace — half an hour's wait for tea and bread and butter!

The little Muswell Hill and Palace Railway remained nominally independent until 14th. August 1911, from which date the Great Northern was able to increase its empire a little further by purchasing it for an outlay of £18,416. Thus, the smaller company was absolved from having to pay for improvements which the GNR had carried out at the Alexandra Palace station, which had survived the first fire and its traffic to that date almost unchanged, though in a state of dilapidation and general torpor. The chief alteration was to shorten the long platform to a point short of the terrace steps.

At the same time as Mr. Hawkins was promoting his developments, including the tramway up the hill, there had appeared in the Parliamentary Session of 1898 a further Bill, whereby the Muswell Hill and Palace Railway sought to reach round once more by a pincer movement from the north side of the Palace to Wood Green, this time taking a slightly more tortuous route nearer to Wood Green itself, then over the tunnel and down by flying junctions to the GN main line and the awaiting stub end of the GE Palace Gates branch. Railway No. 1 was to commence from the original branch near the north east end of Alexandra Palace and run north, then north west round the ornamental lake, crossing the football ground and then turning east to a point south west of Edith Road, a small thoroughfare which actually lay in the straight line of any projection north west of the Palace Gates branch. Quite a lot of railway land was available hereabouts, some of it taken up by the junction used by the Gordon Hill and Enfield trains. Railway No. 2 was to be the spur running south from the main line at the Edith Road junction, to the down side of the Enfield branch. Railway No. 3 was simply the other side of the flying junction connecting with the Up line of the Enfield branch on one side of the bridge carrying Bridge Road over the GN line at Wood Green station. Railway No. 4 was to be a double line connecting into the Palace Gates branch at an end-on junction at a point opposite the northern end of the Down platform at Palace Gates station.

Additionally, the Company were to apply for powers for lands 'situate on the north side of the northern fence of the Alexandra Palace station of the M H & P R and extending from the western side of The Avenue leading to the north terrace of Alexandra Palace for a distance of 280 yd. or thereabouts in length, measured in a south westerly direction; such piece of land to be of a width of 47 yd. or thereabouts.' Rather cryptic, this latter parcel of land was possibly an investment on which to site either more lavish station buildings, or more likely a goods yard, since one was missing from the original layout.

Development continued along the Muswell Hill road, especially to the east and south of the branch. Business was forthcoming and a third station, Cranley Gardens, was opened on 2nd. August 1902, named after one of the original lanes on the hill. Shops and other amenities opened, along with the customary 'Broadway', and a regular clientele was assured for the line, with a brisk traffic in building supplies running to Muswell Hill station yard where a network of light railways transported supplies directly to the building sites.

This time of glory for the little branch lasted perhaps five years in all, for by December 1905 the new electric tram had found its way up the hill to the palace, terminating provocatively just south of the Great Northern station and parallel to it. The cars ran from Turnpike Lane, while from April of the next year a similar service ran up to the east entrance, both routes with their hills being ideal for the new traction.

The electric cars were tolerable perhaps, but less acceptable were the dreaded motor omnibuses which the London General Omnibus Company ran, single deckers from Finsbury Park to Muswell Hill with an ominously frequent service from Highgate to the same spot.

A clever blocking move by the GN which was partially successful was to complain of the damage done by the buses to overbridges at Cranley Gardens and Crouch End stations, which led to the imposition of weight restriction on the road vehicles.

The Alexandra Palace branch kept its regular patrons, however, and indeed did quite well from Sunday School outings, festivals and rallies where vast crowds could be catered for more expeditiously than by tram or bus. A rally on 15th. November 1913 was attended by Winston Churchill.

On the outbreak of the Great War everything changed. The Palace closed on 8th. August 1914 and was then commandeered for use in assembling reservists who arrived on rail vouchers. After these came the solemn trek of refugees from the theatre of war on the Continent, brought to the Palace by special trains direct from the Channel ports and Tilbury. The third phase began in 1915 when enemy prisoners were interned at the Palace. A report of the situation there on Christmas Eve 1915 found accommodation available for 3,500 prisoners, but at no time did the number present on role exceed 2,115. The food was excellent, with plenty of home made bread and doughnuts. The trustees lost no time in presenting an exhibition of toys and craftwork made by the prisoners who seem to have had quite a splendid time. Along with them could be found emigrants frozen in transit, as it were. One noteworthy, touching story of the Great War is that of the vessel 'Amiral Gauteaume' which struck a mine on 28th. October 1914 on its way from Calais to Le Havre while carrying 2,500 French refugees. Almost all of these were picked up by the South Eastern Railway ferry 'Queen' plying between Folkestone and Boulogne and ultimately over 1,000 of the survivors were housed in neat rows of beds in the Great Hall of the often maligned but here exceedingly useful Palace.

After hostilities had finished, a whole host of civil servants moved in to take part in the administrative work needed to set things back on their normal course again, though life was never again quite as before. The Palace opened again in 1922, two years after the Park. Its return to the life of entertainment was celebrated by more rallies and the like, and one event drew 60,000, a brave echo of the days of the past. During all these comings and goings the railway passenger service had carried on, though cut back to and from Finsbury Park in off-peak periods due to the heavy use of the main line for war traffic of all kinds. Sunday trains had been suspended and were not in fact to return until February 1925 after a lapse of ten years. They had vanished altogether by 1931.

The London and North Eastern Railway had been formed in 1923, absorbing many older companies including the Great Northern. The new company did not unduly exert itself to try and develop the traffic potential; perhaps it was scared off by the Underground proposals then in the air. Indeed, the old GN had had dreams of electric trains running to the City, these dating from as early as 1892 when it was proposed to run traffic to or from the traditional outer suburban termini through connections at Drayton Park and Finsbury Park with the Great Northern and City Railway to Moorgate. These were partially constructed, but ultimately abandoned because of quarrels over finance. The LNER did in fact look again at the proposal in 1924, but found it overshadowed by the scheme which would extend the Piccadilly Line to Cockfosters, which secured great support.

In 1927 the North London Home Life Exhibition was held from 9th. to 19th. February, earlier than the seasonal opening. The stability of life in those days was reflected in the admission charge of one shilling, which included free travel to the Park on all trams in the North London district. On the LNER it was not quite so easy to obtain concessions, though if one presented oneself at Messrs. Barton and Co.'s premises in Wood Green, it was possible to secure a voucher which allowed single fare prices for the return journey up to ten miles from the Park. Quite obviously it was just not worth the trouble with all the trams clattering up and down offering free rides.

The darker and more facetious aspect of affairs was again reflected in readers' letters to local newspapers, though no less than 'The Observer'

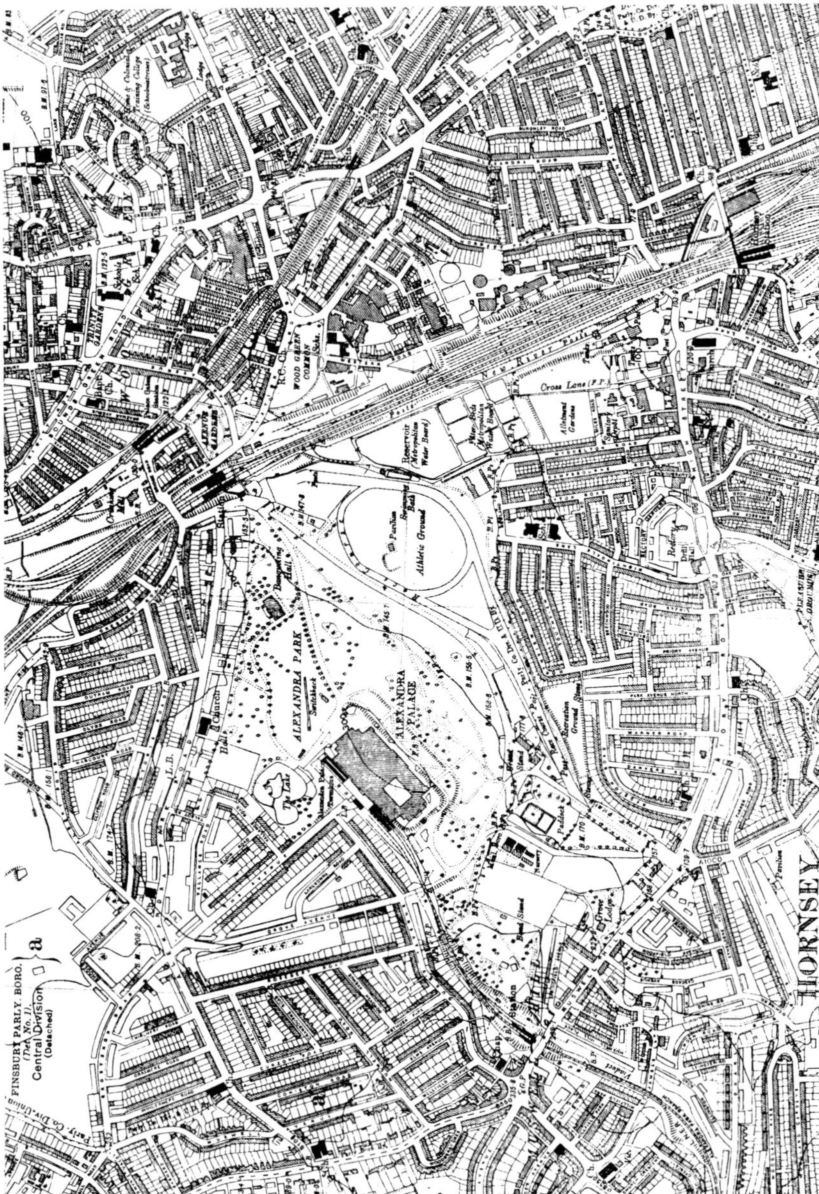

A Palace in Suburbia — 1930s.

carried such an item on 25th. November 1928 which might evoke an impression not wholly unfair. The headline reads 'The Monster of Muswell Hill' and the initial comments are in answer to one of the periodic pleas by the Trustees for public subscription to defray maintenance costs:–

'What is going to happen? Nothing. We shall go on as before. It is a mystery to this generation that the Crystal Palace should 'go on', but the other palace is a deeper mystery still. Time itself has come to a halt on Muswell Hill, and the nineteenth century has left its body to rot there. Alexandra Palace is pathetic where Crystal Palace is, and always has been, funny. It begins with a deserted railway station which is as drab as only railway stations can be. If you go by the wooden stairway and the dank passage, it is impossible to tell where the station ends and that part of the Palace, which the plan calls 'picture gallery' begins, for they both have the same third class waiting room quality, but after fifty yards or so you come to a vast canvas leaning against the wall, half up and half down which is a copy of a very crowded and naked composition of the Venetian School, and it is astonishing how drab and English the Venetians of the third class waiting room have become. Unfortunately someone has put his foot through one of them.'

To Edgware and Highgate

With electrification on the air, it is opportune to sketch the growth of the major branch, that to Finchley from which the Alexandra Palace line diverged at Highgate.

The Edgeware (sic), Highgate and London Railway gained authority by an Act of 1862 for a line from Seven Sisters Road (Finsbury Park) to Edgware, for which they had the backing of £220,000 capital. To run to Edgware only would have been an act either of blind faith or sheer folly, as the village was small and development far off. From Finchley, therefore, a further branch was sanctioned in July 1866 and opened to High Barnet, a more worthy and vigorous destination, in April 1872. For this reason it was always considered the more important goal for suburban rains. The Midland Railway, which passed close by to the west in the vicinity of Elstree, tried to shake the EH & LR by proposing a branch of their own to Watford, with arms to Highgate and Muswell Hill. This proposal was soon scrapped however, after the Great Northern had taken over the local company in 1867.

Stations on the new line were at Crouch End, Highgate, East End Finchley, Finchley & Hendon and Mill Hill, these being normal in design except for Mill Hill, where one platform served the single line. The line was doubled to East End Finchley in December 1867 and to Finchley & Hendon in November 1869, where some trains were terminated, using an island platform on the down side.

From Finchley the branch ran off to Barnet, double track with stations at Woodside Park and Totteridge which remained a rural backwater until quite late in life. Barnet was 11 miles from King's Cross and 5½ miles from Finchley, while Edgware, equidistant from Finchley, was soon reduced to a sort of poor railway relation with a shuttle service of trains from the junction, though it must be remembered that originally great hopes were held out for the branch, the terminus being built as a through station for a possible extension to Watford.

Finchley was really the major place on the whole network, with a good sized population even in the line's infancy and with over 20,000 at the turn of the century. In February 1887 East End Finchley became East Finchley, and

Waiting to depart from the lee of The Palace.

Finchley & Hendon became Finchley Church End, then Finchley Central. As if this were not confusing enough, a later station, West Finchley, was opened in March 1933, while a halt called Mill Hill, the Hale, was opened adjacent to the overbridge carrying the Midland main line in June 1906. To complete the development of the stations, Stroud Green station was opened adjacent to Crouch Hill on the Tottenham and Hampstead Joint line at the Finsbury Park end of the line on 11th April 1881, replacing a solitary signal box at about the same spot, called 'Reservoir'.

The pattern of train services was originally based on Finchley and Highgate with some workings terminating at these points and returning either to King's Cross or Finsbury Park, or running beyond principally to Edgware in the early days, then to Barnet once it was realised where the revenue lay. Thus, in 1904, whereas some two dozen trains left Edgware in the morning period, of which nearly all ended their journeys at Finchley, fifty came down from High Barnet and ran through, with a further fifty or so from Muswell Hill, of which half would come from Alexandra Palace. Add to all this a sprinkling of short workings from East Finchley and Highgate, and it can soon be imagined how busy such stations could be at rush hours. Some trains had been running through to City stations from 1868.

The Edgware-Finchley shuttle was worked by Ivatt steam rail motors from February 1906 and, for a time in 1929 by the Sentinel steam railcar 'Rising Sun'. Like the Alexandra Palace services, the Edgware/High Barnet trains suffered as soon as the trams began to make inroads into the commuter areas, the first cars running from Highgate to High Barnet in March 1907. However, the GNR put up a good fight with a frequent and reliable service run by the then new, big tank engines, and with reasonable fares. The Great War caused reductions of course, for the same reasons as those which had affected Alexandra Palace traffic, namely wartime pressure on the main line and widened lines which suspended through running to Moorgate and Broad Street.

The LNER found itself with an embarrassment of suburban traffic, a heavy burden which it could not really handle properly, offering to its customers the grim articulated stock which compared badly with some of the admittedly old but nevertheless relatively luxurious saloons offered to Great Eastern clientele using Palace Gates station; but even in their regimentation and matchwood they were better by far then the abominable LMS 4 wheelers which found their way up from Broad Street.

London Transport New Works

The Plan of 1935 would have radically altered the basis of train operation over the three branches, as it proposed that all the commuter traffic should be taken over by electrified extensions of London Transport. However, much of this advance planning was scotched because of the outbreak of the second World War, and works that had been started were in some cases left in suspended animation and abandoned when peace returned.

A foretaste of what was to come was the resignalling of the section from Finsbury Park No. 7 signal box to Highgate Park Junction by the LNER with colour light signals in 1932, though this only gave a slightly more up-to-date efficiency to a hard worked steam line.

Simply, the 1935 plan involved the extension of the Northern Line underground route from Archway station to a surface station at East Finchley, whence it would use the existing lines to Barnet and Edgware.

Next, the Great Northern and City would have its extension from Drayton Park to a new platform at Finsbury Park, with electric trains running to Highgate where a two level exchange station would be built. From here the trains would run, not to East Finchley, as that portion of track from Park Junction would be obsolete, but up to Alexandra Palace. There is no doubt that if these ideas had been expedited more quickly, the route to the palace would still be doing business today.

During the thirties, traffic to the pleasure grounds was fairly even, with the North London Exhibition attracting 300,000 in 1932, and with 5,000 Wood Green children enjoying an old fashioned treat in 1933. In the same year the Trustees again called for more public financial support for little cash was available to keep out the damp and no doubt the naked Venetians in the 3rd. class waiting room were by now almost in extremis.

A Modernisation Plan for the palace was also published. This envisaged replacing the ebullient Victorian decor by vistas of chromium, mirrors and glass. Happily, the ideas were not implemented. The Willis organ remained undisturbed, but possibly registered a certain surprise at the goings-on in part of the building where the new television was being reviewed and tested on 12th. September 1936. The East wing was used for BBC purposes, with early transmissions of two hours daily going out to receivers within a 25 miles radius.

On 5th. August 1938 the Palace almost suffered a similar fate to its predecessor and Crystal Palace which had been destroyed in 1936, had not a Hornsey fireman on sick leave been walking with his family in the grounds and heard crackling sounds. He suspected fire and on investigation found a scullery and store room ablaze, which was dealt with very promptly.

It was not possible to arrange a physical rail connection at Highgate due to the difference in levels. Had this been contrived, then the low level line would have also been able to run direct to the Palace. The original Northern Line underground terminated just beyond the platform ends at Highgate station. One of the stubs was extended through to East Finchley, while the other was used for reversing purposes. This took place some eighty feet below the LNER line, and opportunity was taken to construct a new, combined booking office below the LNER platforms. This meant that some of the old surface buildings were demolished, and staircases linked the surface platforms to the new lower booking hall, while from here escalators would take passengers to or from the Archway road 60 ft. above.

At Highgate the Wellington carriage sidings were adapted for tube rolling stock, and further accommodation was sited in the angle between the Alexandra Palace branch and main line. The LNER coaching stock formerly here was moved to Bounds Green (Palace Gates) in a shed paid for by London Transport, while the Royal train which had its home at Highgate, was moved to Doncaster.

There were engineering difficulties posed by bringing the Northern Line to the surface at East Finchley, as it was necessary firstly to honour the existing level at Highgate (Archway) station and then to come up level with the LNER to cross the Great North Road on a common alignment. It was possible to make do with a 1 in 50 maximum rise for down trains, but 1 in 40 for southbound trains, as these had the additional complication of having to burrow beneath the LNER line. Due to land use and the proximity of the surface railway, here on an embankment, the tunnel mouths had to be constructed in a special manner which dispensed with a bell mouth entrance, and southbound trains entered a tightly fitting concrete chamber ahead of the tunnel proper which had a series of fifteen closely set air vents like holes in a flute to release the air pressure caused by the piston effect of an entering train.

Traffic continued to be brisk on the two branches, with 57 trains from High Barnet each day alone in 1938, and some eight goods trains on both branches; one tends to forget these latter workings which could cause operating headaches at times. The single line to Edgware had 26 trains each way daily in the same year.

War clouds in the air did not prevent underground services to Finchley

H.C. CASSERLEY

A Moorgate-bound train arriving at Stroud Green.

Crouch End Station looking towards Highgate in G.N.R. days.

Highgate slumbering in an off-peak mist.

from being started from 3rd. July 1939, and to High Barnet on 14th. April 1940. At once, the improvements offered to passengers were enormous, with over 200 electric workings replacing the 57 steam ones from High Barnet, and a ten minute service at peak hours and five minutes at Finchley.

Edgware was caught out by the war, however, and while the section from Finchley was in fact closed from 11th. September 1939 for doubling, nevertheless the work which had in fact started in November 1936 was never completed and the best that could be done was to send tube trains out along the single line to Mill Hill East, where a large barracks were situated, from 18th. May 1941. The run of line gave a direct service across London to Morden at most times of the day. Edgware was reached directly by another route, a branch of the Northern Line from Camden Town via Golders Green, but the station was still linked to Mill Hill East for many years by the old single line which carried a goods service, steam operated, to serve Edgware coal sidings, the Middlesex Gasworks at Mill Hill East and the United Dairies Creamery at East Finchley.

During the Second World War Alexandra Palace was again used for military purposes, and saw thousands of refugees from Malta and Gibraltar. It also offered welcome storage space for loads of furniture deposited there from bombed out homes in the area. Not every part of the park was closed, for the roller skating drome continued to operate for the duration, and gave pleasure to many, including servicemen on leave.

Once the war came again, and when the Underground had reached Archway and Mill Hill, through workings to and from the City and Broad Street ceased.

At the beginning of the war trains ran to and from Finsbury Park, timetabled during the morning and evening rush hour and on an al fresco basis during the rest of the time when a 'frequent service' of unspecified trains was offered to fit in with war traffic, bomb damage and the like.

After 7th. September 1942, the service was cut to three per hour between Finsbury Park and Alexandra Palace at peak times, with an embargo on trains after 7 p.m. weekdays and 5 p.m. on Saturdays, a truly rural sort of existence. There was a rather nasty gap during the slack period which persisted as the branch dreamed on up to the early fifties, when it was narrowed to a long lunch break of four hours between 11.30 a.m. and 3.30 p.m.

Like others of its kind, the little branch was something of an anachronism and, embarrassed by it, British Railways were only too ready to make its ife difficult. Shortage of manpower caused a temporary closure from 27th. October 1951 to 1st. January 1952, with a resumption in the shape of 17 up and 15 down trains, including a couple of short workings to Highgate and back. The lunch break was now extended from 9.42 a.m. to 5.05 p.m. Saturday services were similar, but with a close-down after the last up train had left Alexandra Palace at 5.25 p.m.

Of course, much of this operation was largely a matter of keeping staff happy and the rails free from rust, as many commuters had already taken to the No. 212 bus. However, London Transport had included Alexandra Palace in its fare calculations, as the station could be quoted from anywhere in the city. Based on mileage, however, the rate to the Palace showed up badly compared with the fare to Wood Green. By closure on 5th. June 1954 there was a shuttle service of two-coach trains making twelve round trips, the average loading never exceeding more than fifty passengers, with half that number on Saturdays.

Following the closure of the Alexandra Palace branch to passengers, the line was successively cut back to Muswell Hill station which became a railhead for coal, and where a conveyor belt of advanced design was installed in April 1961, and subsequently the line was only traversed as far as Cranley Gardens by a goods train which left Highbury at 11.30 a.m. Goods traffic on the branches had been building materials, coal and what are always called sundries, and these diverse commodities had been carried by eight or nine goods workings up and down. Special needs were presented by the Middlesex Gasworks at Mill Hill, with the barracks nearby, and also by the United Dairies milk factory at East Finchley, to which point Staffordshire milk had been brought nightly. This traffic ceased in 1948, while the gas works closed in 1961. Occasionally, as on 25th. June 1932, special trains would appear at Mill Hill for the Hendon Air Show.

From 1956 there were still quite a few goods workings out to East Finchley and beyond, with severe limitation of loading, due to the gradients and age of the engines involved, which reduced the maximum size of trains to 14 loaded wagons. Basically there were nine goods trains out to East Finchley, and most of these went beyond. Four of them carried coal for the gas works. The first outward goods was the 6.55 a.m. from Highbury to Highgate Yard, followed by the 8.40 a.m. from Highbury running non-stop to Woodside Park and Totteridge, arriving at High Barnet at 11.35 a.m. This working then set off on the return trip at 2.15 p.m., again running non-stop to Highbury which it reached at 2.52 p.m. Next came one of the Edgware goods workings, the 8.10 a.m. from King's Cross with loaded wagons out and empties for return. The fourth working was the 10.02 a.m. Highbury to East Finchley, Finchley Central and Mill Hill East, followed by the first of the gas coal trains, the 10.35 a.m. down. This and the other three workings at 11.02 a.m., 6.30 p.m. and 8.00 p.m. would be held at East Finchley until a suitable path could be found for them among the Underground trains.

The single line to Mill Hill was controlled from Finchley Central signal box, and officially the steam engines could respond to the trip cocks actuated by the colour light signals en route. In practice, however, there were difficulties. The two goods which ran beyond Mill Hill East to the terminus needed the key to the Edgware ground frame to manipulate the sidings. The second of these trains left Highbury at 12.52 p.m. with coal, then the engine would shunt the extensive sidings during the afternoon and set out on the return trip at 6.30 p.m. with whatever had been collected. Coal and bricks from Fletton, Peterborough, were the main inward loads, and trains were made up at Highbury or Clarence Yards. Finchley Central handled single items which could be transferred to road there.

Some interesting old engines worked the A.P. branch, including N1 and N2 class tanks, N7 tanks of Great Eastern origin, the asthmatic C12s, of which 67536 was a regular performer, and the last Great Central Class F2, 2-4-2T No. E7111 which breathed its last in December 1950. The last passenger train to Alexandra Palace ran on 3rd. July 1954, a rake of gaslit stock headed appropriately by an N2 which set the seal on the proceedings by breaking down and having to be pushed along by a fellow engine off the next down freight.

Steam workings stopped in 1961, when diesel power took over, but a general closure of goods yards took place in October 1962, though those at Finchley, The Hale and Edgware continued until 1964, and the line west of Mill Hill East was lifted in the following September.

N.E. STEAD

G.N. 4–4–2T No 67374 at Muswell Hill on a branch working.

A train headed by a N2 tank engine arriving at Muswell Hill in British Railways' days.

Looking Ahead

The most recent development in the story of Alexandra Palace has been the important adoption of the building and park by Haringey Council, the whole of the site and structures being handed over to them by the Greater London Council as from January 1980, together with a dowry of £8½ million. Details of the many problems to be solved before the palace could be considered to be in a presentable state, together with a potted history, were contained in an excellent illustrated report issued by the GLC Alexandra Palace Working Party in October 1979. The list of items removed, deteriorating or destroyed over the years is impressive, though the most important one to most readers, the station, is not given a mention. Thirteen such have disappeared from the park alone, including the race course and its accessories and no less than eleven tennis courts. However, the GLC spent over £1,268,000 in maintenance since they took over in 1966, rising from £30,000 in 1966/7 to £182,000 in 1977/8. Currently in residence are departments of the Middlesex Polytechnic and the BBC, who, it is hoped, will be vacating the East wing in 1982. As well as these long staying guests, many other temporary ones come to exhibitions, concerts, rallies, banquets and the like, and the Great Hall and Palm Court are each licensed to hold 6,000 and 1,000 guests respectively. In 1979 the Great Hall was on hire for 63.7% of the total available time, which could be brought up to 85% with careful planning. Income from hire in 1979 was £218,000. Remembering the ghosts of happy thousands who attended on those sunny Bank Holidays many years ago, comparable figures for 1979 were 127,000 visiting the Custom Car Show in one week, and 30,000 for a Jazz Festival. Catering for banquets held in two rooms brought in £450,000. The park brings in little, except about £800 per month from putting greens.

Looking ahead, what is envisaged is a modernised Great Hall with a solid load bearing floor and better access for the unloading and loading of exhibits as well as new dining areas and bars, a 120 bedroom hotel, restaurant and lounge. Radio links would not cease, however, as Decca Radio have shown themselves interested in setting up a recording studio and theatre in the north west tower.

What of the organ? Much of the bits and pieces left are currently held at Henry Willis's works in Petersfield, and it could be restored with an electric blower at a cost of £250,000.

No longer will crowds toil up the hill by train and tram. Most arrive by car, and there will be places for 2,882 cars, plus 66 coaches. Access roads will cope with flows of up to 1,600 vehicles per hour.

Bus services will be covered by a strengthened W3 route. An extension of the 251 Eastern National Southend service to the palace is envisaged.

Rail passengers will use Wood Green station, renamed Alexandra Palace in May 1982, with the inducement of cheap facilities to and from the West End, not exactly a bumper offering in view of the distance between the station and palace; one assumes that they will be duly warned of the need to transfer to the W3 bus, a retrograde step after the earlier luxury of a station under the palace walls.

The Planning Report has the last word, in language which could have been read in documents produced at any time during the palace's history:

'Monorails, funicular railways and other means of movement have been investigated, but the high capital costs outweigh the benefits to be obtained for the fluctuating use being made of Alexandra Palace and Park. There may, however, be some scope for reintroducing historic forms of transport as an added attraction to visitors.'

However the ink on the foregoing manuscript was scarcely dry when the Palace suffered yet another major misfortune, on 10th. July 1980 when the building brought some 300 firemen to Muswell Hill to tackle a blaze which began at 2.40 p.m., possibly started in a way which shows history repeating itself, when workmen were using blowlamps to strip paint from the Willis organ in the Great Hall. All that now survives of the latter are some thirty five tall pewter pipes. In all, some three fifths of the building were destroyed, the

TED STORMER

Fire Appliances in Action, 10th July 1980

Great Hall itself where the fire began being reduced to a shell with the outside walls threatening to collapse.

Television news reports of the sad event were conveyed with an air of almost indecent glee, as if one of the momentous firework displays were taking place in the grounds. Not so gleeful perhaps would be the insurance companies involved, as Haringey Council had insured the structure for £31 million, with the BBC in adjoining studios for a further £16 million. The Council increased the cover substantially after purchasing the premises from the Greater London Council for a nominal £1.

In spite of everything it is proposed to go ahead with a projected development of the site as a conference and leisure centre with an initial outlay of £30 million. By coincidence, the insurance assessors estimated the total damage at £31 million, a staggering figure only exceeded by the sum of £72.5 million lost at British Aerospace, Weybridge in January 1980. A public inquiry into this ambitious 'phoenix' project is being held in the former BBC premises in the East Wing. Although a poll of Haringey residents showed 71% in favour of the Council's scheme there are numerous and vociferous objectors for the proposals — many want a development smaller in scale and attracting fewer people. At present the only active and slightly incongruous elements alive on the Palace eminence are a shell like modern hall used for the sale of cheap clothes and such, a dry ski-run and ironically enough, tucked under the lee of the ruin alongside the old station a British Rail research building!

BRITISH BROADCASTING CORPN

The Dawn of T.V. — Studio A at the Palace, August 1936.

The Railway Described

From Finsbury Park the locomotive, usually a superannuated tank engine of honourable lineage, found the heavy gradient of 1 in 60 somewhat formidable, passing through the wayside stations of Stroud Green and Crouch End, the latter with side platforms linked by a road bridge at the west end which carried the booking office. Behind the southern platform was a single siding which was controlled by a small signal box on the up side. At 2¼ miles from Finsbury Park the train entered Highgate station after running through one of a pair of rather tight fitting single track tunnels, each of 139 yd. Here the station was of an island construction with a central footbridge linking it to both sides of the railway. After the end of hostilities in 1945 there was a curious atmosphere here of ancient and modern, with old E H & L woodwork cheek by jowl with brash London Transport concrete, the whole set in a wooded cutting out of which the shell of an unfinished escalator shaft emerged. The business part of Highgate lay south west of the line, which was paralleled by Archway Road, along which trams ran in competition. The station enjoyed some importance and was considered as a potential terminus for local services as early as 1901. On the up side was the open area of Highgate Wood.

Still climbing, the train entered a second tunnel, again one of a pair, each of 332 yd., and reached Park Junction signal box sited on the left where the Alexandra Palace branch diverged to the right. In the fork were the LNER carriage sheds of eight roads, plus a couple of long sidings where the Royal train was housed from time to time. Later, this site was used to store Underground trains. Beyond the line to Finchley was the Wellington Sidings, referred to earlier.

From the Park Junction the climb continued at 1 in 95 easing to 1 in 240 at a height of about 236 ft., as the line curved round Highgate Wood with glimpses of housing development on the left hand or western side. The first station on the branch at the north east corner of the wood was Cranley Gardens, quite rural with trees and beds of flowers, situated to the west of Muswell Hill road and south of Woodside avenue. Nearby was Woodside Hospital, and a small reservoir. The station was a fairly simple affair, with

Palace Station shortly before Closure.

69576 simmers on a wet day at the Palace.

small buildings of wood and brick and with the main booking office on the overbridge, from which ramps led down to the platforms. Until closure the stations sported gaslamps, and of course the colour light signals had not penetrated as far as this, though the groundwork of LT electrification was evident in the shape of odd cables here and there. South of the station was the goods yard of three roads, connected to the up line and supervised by the signal box on the down side. Adjacent to this was a short spur which ran to the pump house serving the aforesaid reservoir. The station master of Cranley Gardens also latterly supervised Muswell Hill, and shuttled to and fro between the two. Now running due east, the train entered a cutting and then emerged, on to the seventeen arch span of St. James Lane viaduct, a not too elegant brick affair but one which boasted quite acceptable views over the numerous housetops. On it the line swung round to the north and entered Muswell Hill station, set in a deepish cutting with a road overbridge at the London end from which ramps led down from the booking office alongside it. At the country end of the station the platforms were spanned by an open footbridge leading passengers northwards and homewards by a private pathway to a network of avenues and the vicinity of the original Mus Well.

It will be remembered that the cutting here was a slippery one, and on its edge on the west side clung a hotel jostling with a Baptist church, while to the east lay the park with a convenient entrance off Springfield Avenue hard by. Really there was little need, if one were at all fit, to take the train right to the terminus, as the walk up through the lawns, past the serried ranks of public toilets, the band stand and tennis courts was pleasant enough. Muswell Hill station was the busiest on the line and was given a passimeter booking office in 1927. There was a small goods yard of two roads behind the up platform under the eye of the signal box on the down, while on the down side beyond the station were a couple of long sidings in which stock could be stored and run round, said to be the original stabling point of the private Muswell Hill Company's engine.

By now the park would be in full view. The line turned north east and, at the point where the long sidings trailed in there was a scissors crossover, the double track swinging over an avenue into the grounds and entering the area of Alexandra Palace station.

Originally the terminus was a wooden affair of three platforms, the departure line being served by two faces and the whole being well peppered with gas lamps. Two early photographs show both the station and the ruins of the first palace very clearly; this was built fairly well back from the railway which lay below a sloping bank, while access to the palace was by steps and a terrace span at right angles to the line and roughly half way along the platforms. This distance from the palace more than likely saved the station from similar destruction by the flames and it continued in its original form until the turn of the century. When the new palace was built, its north wall came up close to the line and in due course the layout was then changed to its final form with a basic long island platform running as far as the limits set earlier. No turntable was provided here, though, it will be recalled, one was requested in the original specifications.

For the original layout a signal box was provided off the platform end and a scissors crossing was immediately beyond it. Adjacent to the palace was a short road probably used for standing one or two coal wagons for heating the boilers.

Two sidings were added to the north side of the layout at a later date and these too survived subsequent remodelling.

Eventually the island platform was shortened back to where the steps and approach crossed the line, and umbrella roofed buildings were provided with a small booking office building facing the approach road. The scissors crossover was moved away from the platform ends, and a new signal box with a domestic type roof was provided on the down side. One road was left parallel to the departure platform under the palace wall. This had a small loading dock for palace use at the buffer stop end, and a crossover enabled the train engine to run round its coaches. In later years the arrival side of the island was hardly used. Great Northern somersault signals remained to the end, with a three way bracket for approaching traffic and the two departure signals on a wide bracket.

Following the takeover by the Great Northern of the Muswell Hill and Palace Company, the former soon realised that certain repairs had to be carried out to bring the acquired line up to standard. On 9th. January 1913 an internal letter was written from Mr. C. Brown, the GN Engineer to the Way and Works Committee:

'Alexandra Palace station, when taken over by us, was in such a bad state of repair that the reconstruction or removal of a portion of it has become necessary. Under the terms of clause 77 of our Act of 1911 we have powers to remove those portions of the terrace giving access to our lines. The terrace consists of iron girders with heavy jack arches between, and is laid out on top with a roadway and turf. It is difficult to keep watertight, and as the Company is responsible for maintenance, I would recommend its removal to the extent indicated to reduce future expense.

The Platform adjoining the Palace, and the roof over the same with buildings at the end of the platform, and also the verandah over the north end of the island platform are not required for traffic purposes, and I propose to remove them, using material recovered for repairing the verandah roof at the southern end of the platform, and making good the blank between that roof and that part of the terrace which is to remain.

'A siding is to be laid for the stabling of coaches, as the station is used for the storage of branch trains overnight.'

The estimate of the cost was £1,524, plus £289 for the siding. Tenders received ranged from £4,485 to Messrs. Dolman & Sons of £1,919. The dearest could not offer a completion date. The latter offered 16 weeks and secured the contract.

After complete closure nature soon took over the abandoned trackbed but with a rare stroke of imagination it has now been turned into a footpath where one can escape into countryside just a few miles from Central London.

Bus services were strengthened locally, with up to 46 journeys per hour using single deck vehicles, double deckers taking over at a slightly greater headway when the bridge at Muswell Hill was filled in. This removed a long standing limitation on bus weights. Another difficulty which is still literally unsurmountable in bad weather at times is the 1 in 9 gradient of Muswell Hill itself. For thirteen years an express bus was tried on the route, offering a flat fare of 6d.

After 1969 flat fare buses were operating at 18 to the hour during the rush period between Muswell Hill and Finsbury Park, while two services operated 20 vehicles per hour between Muswell Hill and Highgate.

Currently the flat fare pay-as-you-enter buses operate on routes W2 Turnpike Lane–Crouch End–Finsbury Park and W3 Finsbury Park–Alexandra Palace–Wood Green–Northumberland Park, this route circling Alexandra Park and W7 Muswell Hill–Finsbury Park. The 144A service from Lower Edmonton terminates at Muswell Hill Broadway.

Train Services from Alexandra Palace to London. 1914.

Weekdays. Up

Alexandra Palace	dep:			7.55	8.03	8.14	8.26
Muswell Hill	dep:	7.14	7.30	7.57	8.05	8.16	8.28
Cranley Gardens	dep:	7.16	7.32	8.00	8.08	8.19	8.30
Highgate	dep:	7.19	7.35	8.03	8.11	8.22	8.33
Finsbury Park	dep:	7.26	7.42	8.10	8.18	8.29	8.40
Kings Cross	arr:	7.32M	7.56	8.18M	8.28M	8.37	8.48
Moorgate	arr:	—	8.07	—	—	8.48	8.59
Broad Street	arr:	—	—	—	—	—	—

Alexandra Palace	dep:	8.32	8.41	8.50	8.57	9.11	9.15
Muswell Hill	dep:	8.34	8.43	8.52	8.59	9.13	9.17
Cranley Gardens	dep:	8.37	8.46	8.55	9.02	9.15	9.19
Highgate	dep:	8.40	8.49	8.58	9.05	9.19	9.22
Finsbury Park	dep:	8.47	8.56	9.05	9.12	9.26	9.29
Kings Cross	arr:	8.53M	9.04M	9.11M	—	—	—
Moorgate	arr:	—	—	—	—	—	—
Broad Street	arr:	—	—	—	9.27	—	9.43

Alexandra Palace	dep:	9.25	9.44	10.26	10.44	11.34	12.32
Muswell Hill	dep:	9.27	9.46	10.28	10.46	11.36	12.34
Cranley Gardens	dep:	9.30	9.49	10.31	10.49	11.39	12.37
Highgate	dep:	9.33	9.52	10.34	10.52	11.42	12.40
Finsbury Park	dep:	9.40	9.59	10.41	10.59	11.49	12.47
Kings Cross	arr:	9.56	10.05M	10.50M	11.07M	11.58	12.59
Moorgate	arr:	10.07	—	—	—	12.09	1.10
Broad Street	arr:	—	—	—	—	—	—

		SO				SO	SX
Alexandra Palace	dep:	12.57	1.01	1.36	2.11	2.40	2.49
Muswell Hill	dep:	12.59	1.03	1.38	2.13	2.42	2.51
Cranley Gardens	dep:	1.02	1.06	1.41	2.16	2.45	2.54
Highgate	dep:	1.05	1.09	1.44	2.19	2.48	2.57
Finsbury Park	dep:	1.12	1.16	1.51	2.26	2.55	3.40
Kings Cross	arr:	1.22	1.27	2.12	2.34	3.05	3.12M
Moorgate	arr:	1.33	1.38	2.23	2.46	3.16	—
Broad Street	arr:	—	—	—	—	—	—

		SO		SO				
Alexandra Palace	dep:	3.01	3.10	3.38	3.51	4.22	4.4
Muswell Hill	dep:	3.03	3.12	3.40	3.53	4.24	4.4
Cranley Gardens	dep:	3.06	3.15	3.43	3.56	4.27	4.5
Highgate	dep:	3.09	3.18	3.46	3.59	4.30	4.5
Finsbury Park	dep:	3.16	3.25	3.53	4.06	4.37	5.
Kings Cross	arr:	3.29	3.33M	4.02	4.14	4.46	5.
Moorgate	arr:	3.40	—	4.13	4.25	4.57	5.
Broad Street	arr:	—	—	—	—	—	—

		SO			SX		
Alexandra Palace	dep:	4.51	5.19	5.38	5.56	6.17	6.2
Muswell Hill	dep:	4.53	5.21	5.40	5.58	6.19	6.2
Cranley Gardens	dep:	4.56	5.24	5.43	6.01	6.22	6.2
Highgate	dep:	4.59	5.27	5.46	6.04	6.25	6.
Finsbury Park	dep:	5.06	5.34	5.53	6.11	6.32	6.
Kings Cross	arr:	—	5.44	6.04SX	6.19	6.47M	6.
Moorgate	arr:	—	5.55SO	6.15SX	6.30	—	7.
Broad Street	arr:	5.27	—	—	—	—	—

				SX			S
Alexandra Palace	dep:	6.33	6.56	7.17	7.36	8.12	8.
Muswell Hill	dep:	6.35	6.58	7.19	7.38	8.14	8.
Cranley Gardens	dep:	6.38	7.01	7.22	7.41	8.17	8.
Highgate	dep:	6.41	7.04	7.25	7.44	8.20	8.
Finsbury Park	dep:	6.48	7.11	7.32	7.51	8.27	8.
Kings Cross	arr:	6.59MSO	—	7.47	8.00	—	—
Moorgate	arr:	7.10SX	—	7.58	8.11	—	—
Broad Street	arr:	—	—	—	—	8.43	8.

Alexandra Palace	dep:	8.41	9.20	9.47	10.19	10.43	11
Muswell Hill	dep:	8.43	9.22	9.49	10.21	10.45	11
Cranley Gardens	dep:	8.46	9.25	9.52	10.24	10.48	11
Highgate	dep:	8.49	9.28	9.55	10.27	10.51	11
Finsbury Park	dep:	8.56	9.35	10.02	10.34	10.58	11
Kings Cross	arr:	9.08M	9.43	10.10	10.40M	—	11
Moorgate	arr:	—	9.54	—	—	—	11
Broad Street	arr:	—	—	—	—	—	-

lexandra Palace	dep:	—
Iuswell Hill	dep:	12.24a.m.
ranley Gardens	dep:	12.26
Iighgate	dep:	12.29
insbury Park	dep:	12.36
ings Cross	arr:	12.42M
Ioorgate	arr:	—
road Street	arr:	—

Sundays. Up

lexandra Palace	dep:	—	—	—	—	—	—
uswell Hill	dep:	10.14a.m.	1.42	3.00	3.50	5.11	6.00
ranley Gardens	dep:	10.16	1.44	3.02	3.52	5.13	6.02
ighgate	dep:	10.19	1.47	3.05	3.55	5.16	6.05
insbury Park	dep:	10.26	1.54	3.12	4.02	5.23	6.12
ings Cross	arr:	10.35	2.06	3.25	4.10	5.35	6.20
oorgate	arr:	—	2.14	3.33	—	5.43	—
road Street	arr:	—	—	—	—	—	—

lexandra Palace	dep:	—	—	—	—
Iuswell Hill	dep:	7.18	8.44	9.32	10.30
ranley Gardens	dep:	7.20	8.46	9.34	10.32
Iighgate	dep:	7.23	8.49	9.37	10.35
insbury Park	dep:	7.30	8.56	9.44	10.42
ings Cross	arr:	7.42	9.08	9.53	10.48
Ioorgate	arr:	7.50	9.16	—	—
road Street	arr:	—	—	—	—

Weekdays Down.

Broad Street	dep:	—	—	7.57	—	—	8.42
Moorgate	dep:	—	7.27	—	8.16	8.30	—
Kings Cross	dep:	5.22	7.38	—	8.27	8.41	—
Finsbury Park	dep:	5.35	7.49	8.13	8.35	8.49	8.56
Highgare	dep:	5.45	7.59	8.23	8.45	8.56	—
Cranley Gardens	dep:	—	8.02	8.26	8.48	—	—
Muswell Hill	dep:	5.49	8.04	8.28	8.50	9.01	9.10
Alexandra Palace	arr:	—	—	—	8.52	—	9.12

Broad Street	dep:	—	—	—	—	—	—
Moorgate	dep:	8.51	—	9.53	10.24	—	11.43
Kings Cross	dep:	9.02	—	10.05	10.35	11.35	11.55
Finsbury Park	dep:	9.12	9.18	10.13	10.43	11.44	12.06
Highgate	dep:	—	—	10.23	10.53	11.54	12.16
Cranley Gardens	dep:	—	9.31	10.26	10.56	11.57	12.19
Muswell Hill	dep:	9.23	9.33	10.28	10.58	11.59	12.21
Alexandra Palace	arr:	9.25	9.35	10.30	11.00	12.01	12.23

		SO		SO	SO		
Broad Street	dep:	—	—	—	—	—	—
Moorgate	dep:	—	12.37	12.55	1.13	1.19	1.36
Kings Cross	dep:	12.23	12.48	1.06	1.24	1.30	1.47
Finsbury Park	dep:	12.29	12.55	1.18	1.30	1.41	1.56
Highgate	dep:	12.39	1.05	1.28	1.40	1.51	2.06
Cranley Gardens	dep:	12.42	1.08	1.31	1.43	1.54	2.09
Muswell Hill	dep:	12.44	1.10	1.33	1.45	1.56	2.11
Alexandra Palace	arr:	12.46	1.12	1.36	1.47	1.58	2.13

		SO		SO	SO	
Broad Street	dep:	—	—	—	—	—
Moorgate	dep:	—	1.59	—	—	—
Kings Cross	dep:	2.02	2.10	2.24	2.33	2.48
Finsbury Park	dep:	2.10	2.17	2.30	2.41	2.56
Highgate	dep:	2.20	2.27	2.40	2.51	3.06
Cranley Gardens	dep:	2.23	2.30	2.43	2.54	3.09
Muswell Hill	dep:	2.25	2.32	2.45	2.56	3.11
Alexandra Palace	arr:	2.28	2.34	2.47	2.58	3.14

		SO	SO		SO		SX
Broad Street	dep:	—	—	—	3.41	—	—
Moorgate	dep:	2.44	—	3.22	—	3.49	4.10
Kings Cross	dep:	2.55	3.08	3.33	—	4.00	4.22
Finsbury Park	dep:	3.04	3.18	3.40	3.55	4.08	4.29
Highgate	dep:	3.14	3.28	3.50	4.05	4.18	4.39
Cranley Gardens	dep:	3.17	3.31	3.53	4.08	4.21	4.42
Muswell Hill	dep:	3.19	3.33	3.55	4.10	4.23	4.44
Alexandra Palace	arr:	3.22	3.36	3.57	4.13	4.25	4.46

							SX	SO
Broad Street	dep:	—	—	—	—	—	—	—
Moorgate	dep:	—	—	—	5.19	—	—	—
Kings Cross	dep:	4.30M	4.57	5.12	5.34	5.45	6.09	6.16
Finsbury Park	dep:	4.41	5.05	5.20	5.40	5.52	6.15	6.23
Highgate	dep:	4.51	5.15	5.30	5.50	6.02	6.25	6.33
Cranley Gardens	dep:	4.54	5.18	5.33	5.53	6.05	6.28	6.36
Muswell Hill	dep:	4.56	5.20	5.35	5.55	6.07	6.30	6.38
Alexandra Palace	arr:	4.58	5.22	5.38	5.57	6.09	6.32	6.40

		SX	SX		SO	SX	
Broad Street	dep:	—	6.20	6.29	—	—	6.56
Moorgate	dep:	6.05	—	6.29	—	—	—
Kings Cross	dep:	6.16	—	6.40	—	7.03M	—
Finsbury Park	dep:	6.22	6.34	6.48	7.02	—	7.09
Highgate	dep:	6.32	6.44	6.58	7.13	7.15	7.19
Cranley Gardens	dep:	6.55	6.47	7.01	7.16	7.18	7.22
Muswell Hill	dep:	6.37	6.49	7.03	7.18	7.20	7.24
Alexandra Palace	arr:	6.39	6.51	7.05	7.20	7.22	7.26

			SO	SX				
Broad Street	dep:	—	7.11	—	—	—	—	—
Moorgate	dep:	7.00	—	7.14	7.39	7.52	8.18	8.34
Kings Cross	dep:	7.11	—	7.25	7.50	8.03	8.31	8.46
Finsbury Park	dep:	7.18	7.25	7.41	7.56	8.13	8.37	8.56
Highgate	dep:	7.28	7.35	7.51	8.06	8.23	8.47	9.06
Cranley Gardens	dep:	7.31	7.38	7.54	8.09	8.26	8.50	9.09
Muswell Hill	dep:	7.33	7.40	7.56	8.11	8.28	8.52	9.11
Alexandra Palace	arr:	7.35	7.42	7.58	8.13	8.31	8.55	9.14

Broad Street	dep:	—	—	—	—	—	—	—
Moorgate	dep:	9.02	—	—	—	—	—	—
Kings Cross	dep:	9.23	9.47M	10.08M	10.45M	11.16	11.35M	11.5
Finsbury Park	dep:	9.29	9.55	10.15	10.52	11.24	11.45	12.0
Highgate	dep:	9.39	10.05	10.25	11.02	11.34	11.55	12.1
Cranley Gardens	dep:	9.42	10.08	10.28	11.05	11.37	11.58	12.1
Muswell Hill	dep:	9.44	10.10	10.30	11.07	11.39	12.00	12.1
Alexandra Palace	arr:	9.46	10.12	10.32	11.09	11.41	12.02	—

Sundays Down

Broad Street	dep:	—	—	—	—	—	—
Moorgate	dep:	—	12.55	2.18	—	—	—
Kings Cross	dep:	9.53M	1.12	2.29	3.00M	4.35M	5.25M
Finsbury Park	dep:	9.41	1.18	2.38	3.24	4.43	5.33
Highgate	dep:	9.51	1.28	2.48	3.34	4.53	5.43
Cranley Gardens	dep:	9.54	1.31	2.51	3.37	4.56	5.46
Muswell Hill	arr:	9.56	1.33	2.53	3.39	4.58	5.48
Alexandra Palace	arr:	—	—	—	—	—	—

Broad Street	dep:	—	—	—
Moorgate	dep:	6.06	7.45	—
Kings Cross	dep:	6.17	7.56	—
Finsbury Park	dep:	6.25	8.04	9.03
Highgate	dep:	6.35	8.14	9.13
Cranley Gardens	dep:	6.38	8.17	9.16
Muswell Hill	dep:	6.40	8.19	9.18
Alexandra Palace	arr:	—	—	—

SO: Sats Only
SX Sats Excepted
M: Main Line Platform
MX: Mons Excepted

RALLY ROUND THE PALLY

ALEXANDRA PALACE

SUGAR